Upper Burnside

Tyree's Knob

Old
Burnside

HARRIETTE SIMPSON ARNOW

THE UNIVERSITY PRESS OF KENTUCKY

Endpaper map by William B. Crouch
Lettering by Calvert Guthrie

Research for The Kentucky Bicentennial Bookshelf
is assisted by a grant from the
National Endowment for the Humanities.
Views expressed in the Bookshelf do not
necessarily represent those of the Endowment.

ISBN: 0-8131-0208-1

Library of Congress Catalog Card Number: 77-73699

A statewide cooperative scholarly publishing agency
serving Berea College, Centre College of Kentucky,
Eastern Kentucky University, The Filson Club,
Georgetown College, Kentucky Historical Society,
Kentucky State University, Morehead State University,
Murray State University, Northern Kentucky University,
Transylvania University, University of Kentucky,
University of Louisville, and Western Kentucky University.

Editorial and Sales Offices: Lexington, Kentucky 40506

Contents

Prologue

ANN ARBOR SCHOOLS, like others in Michigan, have long observed Easter with a week's vacation. During the Easter holiday of 1953, Husband took a week of his vacation in order to help take the children on the long-promised and overdue trip to see their grandmother Simpson at Burnside. Illness and vacations elsewhere had kept us away for more than three years. We would also see Lake Cumberland, one of the largest man-made lakes in the United States.

I had tourist material and newspaper clippings describing the dam, Lake Cumberland, and even the changes in Burnside. I knew Lake Cumberland began near the foot of Cumberland Falls and continued past Burnside and on down to Wolf Creek Dam, the largest earth-fill dam in the United States, over a mile long and 240 feet high. The lake it formed was 101 miles long with a shoreline of 1,255 miles. I thus knew everything and was ready to explain all to the children.

A few miles south of Somerset we came to a high bridge across a wide body of still water. "Children," I said, "this is what used to be Cumberland River; after Wolf Creek Dam was finished in 1950 it became Lake Cumberland."

Two voices came in chorus from the back seat: "The sign said 'Pitman Creek.' "

I sat in silent confusion, looking ahead to find Burnside. The children were the sign watchers, the backseat drivers. We passed a line of garish bedspreads flapping in the wind as our daughter said, "Cumberland River Bridge is just ahead. We're almost to Burnside."

We began to cross the long bridge. I could see little of the water near the bridge because of the head-high cement walls on either side of the two-lane road. Far away on the lake I could see here and there the same sort of pleasure craft I had seen in the Detroit River or Lake Erie. Was that point of land Bunker Hill or Bronston? It looked too low for either. I tried to remember the figures I had learned; when the lake was high, as it now appeared to be, the surface of the water was more than 150 feet higher than the average surface of Cumberland River at Burnside had been.

The bridge ended. We were going past the white limestone and red earth of recent excavations. I remembered I had planned to show the children the road to Bronston and tell them it led to Monticello where the stagecoaches used to stay except when they were traveling back and forth to Burnside. I began: "Children, we'll soon be seeing the bridge across the South Fork to Bronston and Monticello. I remember—."

"Oh, Mother."

"Oh, Mothers" came frequently but with different meanings. I knew this one meant I had said something wrong. Our daughter continued, "We passed a sign for Monticello before we crossed the last bridge."

Our son said, "You mean Kentucky 90, don't you?"

I didn't know. The roads out from Burnside used to have names, not numbers, but maybe the Monticello Pike was now Kentucky 90. We were stopping for a red light. There had never been a traffic light in Burnside. I looked out and up to the shoulder of a hill that rose above the town. That must be Tyree's Knob where I had spent my childhood and our mother continued to live. The shape was different; still, no other hill had risen close above upper Burnside, and the redbud and the dogwood were in bloom to make pink and white patches over the hill as they had used to do.

I looked on either side of the road and saw nothing familiar. The light changed. I saw a sign—"Seven Gables Motel." That didn't mean anything. The building was nothing at all like the Seven Gables Hotel I had known in lower Burnside. Was this wide place in the road Burnside? A moment later I was certain. I saw a sign that said: "Grissom and Rakestraw Lumber." There had been a Grissom and Rakestraw Lumber Company in lower Burnside for many years; Grissoms had lived in the town before it had a name.

Past the name I glimpsed stacks of lumber; then both were behind us as we went through a cut several feet deep and made a sharp turn that brought us to a stretch of road with no buildings on either side. I looked out the window to see the lake with a causeway that ended on the side of a round-topped hill. I knew Bunker Hill even with its feet cut off. "Are you driving us to Tateville?" I asked.

The question angered Husband. He had driven around Burnside more than I. "You surely remember," he told me, "that U.S. 27 before reaching Tateville climbed that steep hill out of Burnside."

"We're on U.S. 27 South." "We've not been down in the valley." Our sign watchers sounded certain.

Traffic was heavy and fast, shoulders narrow. There was no turning back until we reached the parking space for a Tateville store. Nearing Burnside from the south, everybody saw the small sign that indicated the junction with another road, unnamed. We turned off here, though I was uncertain of our whereabouts. The cut and the curve for a new U.S. 27 had destroyed the homes that had stood above Antioch Road as it neared the lane I had walked on my way to and from school. Where was the lane?

I at last saw a familiar home ahead and knew we were on Antioch Road. The home belonged to Mrs. Robert Ellnor whom I had known since early childhood. I wanted to stop and speak with her, but now that we were off the main road with no restaurant in sight, the children declared they were starving to death and must have food.

Husband said we couldn't burst in on my old mother with two hungry children expecting food at once.

He turned around and drove back to the Seven Gables Motel where he had seen a restaurant sign. I told him and the children that I wasn't hungry. I planned, while they were eating, to hunt Burnside on foot.

I crossed U.S. 27 and soon found the upper end of a street

with its sidewalk cracked and broken by the roots of old beech and maples. I had known this street as a child, though I had never lived on it. I walked down this sidewalk until I could see across the way a white-painted house which I knew as the place where the Harry Waits had brought up their three children. I wondered if the little log house the elder Waits had built behind their home was still there. They had arranged on the log walls, in cases, and on tables the swords and several varieties of firearms their ancestors had used in colonial wars, the American Revolution, the War of 1812, and later conflicts—all that for the school children and others curious to know what weapons their forebears had used.

The street I was on ended at the first street above the railway that had come through a cut in the hillside below. I turned right and walked to the far end of that street. The homes that stood surrounded by trees and shrubs in large lawns were only on the upper side of the street. All save two had been built before 1900, but still wore their gingerbread, wide verandas, and window shutters with an air of respectability. I had visited in many—some more often than others. I couldn't visit now; the people who had lived in them back in the used-to-be were dead or gone away.

I turned around and walked to the other end of the street, which brought me to the one road that had connected upper Burnside with the lower town by the rivers. I walked on the sidewalk on one side of the uphill road until I reached a side street. Here I stopped. Looking right along the side street I saw the Christian Church, and across from it the building that had once been Dr. Stigall's home and office, one in a row of other homes. Past the far end of this street I could see the Baptist Church. I turned to look up the hill road with homes on one side and on the other, the Methodist Church, the Masonic Temple, and past these the Burnside Graded and High School.

One part of Burnside still existed—the upper town that used to live chiefly from the business and industry in the lower town.

I turned around and followed the road down past the street I had been on, expecting to cross the railway tracks in a cut high on the hillside. Instead of the railway, the downhill road crossed a new road I have never seen. I was standing in the middle, trying to figure out where the passenger station and Burton's Restaurant had been, when a car honked. I scuttled to one side of the road and watched the long car towing a long boat on a trailer disappear around a curve in the new road.

I walked on, remembering that the railway had been moved. I decided after thinking over what I had read that both U.S. 27 and the railway had been moved a short distance up Cumberland River above Burnside. Going on down the hill, I was soon able to walk by the shore of the lake. It lay there, still and blue until I peered into it to see below the blue a murky nothingness.

I walked on down and onto the floating dock, not stopping until I had reached the end. Here the water was deeper, and I could see only murkiness. I looked across and around the lake, wider here. Burnside Veneer Company had been over there at the end of the line of anchored pleasure craft: the company's log boom had been on the South Fork above the steamboat landing. Where was the South Fork? It had flowed from behind Bunker Hill and on into the Cumberland. The rivers were all one now.

"Ma'am."

I turned around. A young man, the dock manager perhaps, spoke kindly, as if to warn a friend: "Be careful, lady. Don't fall in: the water's deep there, and cold. You go down, you might not come up—like that little boy friskin' around here two or three weeks ago."

I thanked the man and promised to be careful, but did not tell him I knew Cumberland River had been cold. This corpse of the Cumberland would be colder.

I looked again and saw a narrow band of shadow on the water by Bunker Hill. Lower Burnside hemmed by hills and river bluffs had been a place of long shadows that came early and stayed late. It was only an hour or so past noon, and the shadow of Bunker Hill lay on the water. The shadow was small now; it would grow longer but never fall so far as when Bunker Hill had stood tall and free of the lake; but it was there. The shadows would not be destroyed.

1

TWO RIVERS AND
A CANEBRAKE

I CANNOT THINK of the Burnside I knew as a child without remembering the rivers at her doorstep. The larger Cumberland was, in spite of her wicked ways, my favorite. This river rises high on the flanks of Pine and Cumberland mountains where rivulets rush down to form larger streams that merge in the valleys to form the creeks of Poor Fork and Clover Fork. Cumberland River is born when these flow together. Gathering tributaries flowing north or south on a curve but always getting back to her western course, the Cumberland loops and twists past Pineville, Barbourville, and Williamsburg. Flowing northward after a long southward swing, she drops 55.5 feet straight down to form what we know as Cumberland Falls, 46 miles above Burnside.

Near the foot of the falls, the Cumberland that used to be lies still and dead because of Wolf Creek Dam, 101 miles downriver. Past the falls the untamed river twisted her way through rock-walled canyons 100 to 500 feet deep and little wider than the riverbed. About nine miles above the mouth of the South Fork, Cumberland River began to roar down Shadowen Shoals, the first of four shoals in which the channel dropped 54 feet within six miles. The last and worst of the four, known as Smith Shoals, was only a short distance above

Burnside. No craft of any description could get up Smith Shoals; several men were drowned and many barges lost while trying to come downstream.

Smith Shoals marked the end of the narrow canyon and the high hills that stood beyond the canyon; as the river flowed southwestward below the shoals, much of the higher land was level to rolling with a scattering of low hills separated by high valleys. There would still be high bluffs above the Cumberland even during her long southwestward swing into Tennessee, but these seldom rose directly above the water; between the cliffs and the Cumberland were floodplains, sometimes on only one side of the water but often on both. Past the lower end of Smith Shoals, the rock wall on the southern side stood away from the water to leave a narrow margin of land. The floodplain widened in the next mile until above the mouth of the South Fork there was room for lower Burnside. Here too the southern bluff above the river had broken down to form a hillside, steep and rocky, but not too precipitous for men to build a road down to the rivers.

The South Fork of Cumberland River, often called "the Big South Fork," had done her share in building a site for Burnside. Rising high on the Cumberland Plateau in Tennessee, she twisted her way downward and northward to Cumberland River, draining an area of about fifteen hundred square miles on the way. She too has been stilled by Wolf Creek Dam throughout her lower course. The South Fork on reaching what was to be Burnside flowed for a short distance behind Bunker Hill before joining the Cumberland; even behind Bunker Hill there was level and sloping land to serve as sites for future businesses.

Many centuries ago much of the land drained by these rivers was inhabited by human beings whose skeletons and scattered artifacts are the only reminders that they lived at all. These first people disappeared; the rivers flowed on through a land empty of people, but covered by one of the finest hardwood forests in the world. There were many varieties of flowers and ferns, and canebrakes by the rivers that fed the buffalo and deer.

2

The Cherokee, though they lived many miles away on the upper tributaries of the Tennessee River, claimed the Cumberland basin as a hunting ground. Two wandering bands of Shawnee tried at different times to settle near the future site of Nashville, but the Cherokee destroyed each settlement. French explorers and hunters were the first white men known to have visited the Cumberland, and then only the lower half. Somebody apparently visited a Shawnee settlement by the river: late-seventeenth-century French maps, though imperfect, show the river under the name of Rivière des Chauouanons.

The Cumberland remained unknown to the English colonists until 1750, when Dr. Thomas Walker, a Virginia land speculator, found and named the upper river.

Less than twenty years later, Long Hunters were around the mouth of the South Fork. We know from the letters these men or their friends wrote to Dr. Lyman C. Draper that they became familiar with Cumberland River and most of her tributaries from the crossing of the Warriors Path on down to the mouth. They mention Cumberland Falls and a station camp near the mouth of the South Fork. They were familiar with the several Indian trails that crisscrossed southcentral Kentucky, and they used one to cross the Cumberland at "Fish" shoals, so named because of an ancient fish trap nearby, but later renamed Smith Shoals.

Judging from the names hunters gave the creeks in this part of Kentucky, wild animals were abundant. Most Burnsiders knew the locations of Fishing Creek, Buck Creek, Otter Creek, Beaver Creek, Turkey Creek, Marrowbone Creek, Elk Spring Valley, and Deer Lick. There are also in Wayne County Deed Book A references to "Buffalo Road," but the name disappeared shortly after settlement.

There are references in the same deed book to another now-vanished road, the Saltpeter Cave Trace. No one knows to which cave it led. Several caves round about were rich in what was known as niter dirt, first found and dug by the Long Hunters who knew how to treat the dirt to make saltpeter, a prime ingredient of the black gunpowder then in use.

Settlement in southcentral Kentucky and the adjacent hills to the east was slow compared to that in the Bluegrass and near the Ohio River. The first known settlers in the locality were the Price brothers, Benjamin and Abraham, who in 1775 took up a boundary of land and built a cabin in what the Long Hunters called the Big Meadow, near present-day Mill Springs in Wayne County, twelve miles from future Burnside. The cabin disappeared, but the land around was known for generations as Prices' Meadows.

We next hear of families on lower Pitman Creek during the hard winter of 1779–1780. Pitman Creek flowed into the Cumberland River from the north, across from and just below the mouth of the South Fork. A few years later, the Hardgroves settled north of the Cumberland, but near the site of Burnside.

During the Revolution, Virginia set aside most of the land in what was then the southern part of Kentucky County, Virginia, as bounty land for the officers and soldiers of the Virginia Line. Most early settlers around future Burnside did not come until after Kentucky had become a state. Many were veterans of the Revolution. More than a hundred years later, the Somerset chapter of the Daughters of the American Revolution established the names of fifty-six veterans of the Revolution who had settled in the county.

The closest settler to future Burnside was Colonel Samuel Newell, who came in 1797 with his wife and a growing family. The Draper manuscripts and other sources tell of his bravery at the Battle of King's Mountain and his later role in the formation of the State of Franklin. He acquired several hundred acres of land that included floodplains on either side of Cumberland River and the western side of the South Fork. He built the family home, named Clio, on the highland above the southern bank of the Cumberland.

Other families by the names of Cowen, Owens, and Hardwick settled along the Cumberland River and the western side of the South Fork, all within a few miles of the mouth of the South Fork. Tates, Sloans, and Stigalls settled further away. Descendants of these families helped build Burnside.

4

John Beaty in 1796 settled south of the Cumberland but on the western side of the South Fork. One of his older sons, William, married and settled east of the South Fork in a bend of the Cumberland above Smith Shoals, only two miles or so from future Burnside with no river between. William Beaty was soon joined by families of Hardgroves, Lewises, Richardsons, and others. The high rolling land above the four shoals became a farming community.

Those who settled before June of 1799 found themselves living in Lincoln County, Kentucky, with the county seat of Stanford fifty miles away. The General Assembly had in 1798 created Pulaski County from parts of Lincoln and Green counties, but the county was not organized until the following year. The assembly appointed justices and named the new county Pulaski in honor of the Polish hero, Count Casimir Pulaski, who was killed during the siege of Savannah in October 1779.

The four justices had to organize a sparsely settled area of sixteen hundred square miles. The first tax list enumerated 383 white males twenty-one years or over, 121 blacks, and 886 horses, while the 1800 census that included women and minors showed 3,100 whites. During the following decades Pulaski increased in population but decreased in size, as chunks were taken to become parts of new counties. (The last cut came in 1912 when McCreary County was formed to leave Pulaski with only 628 square miles.) A dispute over the location of the county seat raged until 1801, when it was at last decided the county town should be located about nine miles north of Cumberland River. The name chosen was Somerset.

Meanwhile, the point of low land at the meeting of the rivers remained the same as when the Long Hunters had found it— except that the buffalo, beaver, deer, and elk were gone. During summers, when the rivers flowed gently, there were small sandy beaches on the southern side of the Cumberland; above these, willows grew on the steep banks that led up to the floodplains. Cane grew thick and tall on the floodplains while giant beech, oak, hickory, sweet gum, and other trees grew on the slopes of the hills above. The silence was broken only by bird song and the wind in the trees.

The fall rains usually began in late autumn. The yearly rainfall was forty-nine inches, most of it between November and April. The rivers swiftened, becoming angry yellow and flecked with foam as they rose until the willows trailed their branches in the water. Most winters or springs brought at least one high tide when the rivers ran through the canebrakes and gnawed at the roots of the trees on the hillside while the willows and saplings ceaselessly lifted their heads from the water, and the river with equal determination rolled over them again.

There was no one there to use the Jacksboro Road, opened in 1804, and passing by only two miles to the south. Built to take horse or ox-drawn wagonloads of iron from the furnaces at Jacksboro, Tennessee, for sale in the Kentucky Bluegrass, use of this road was limited because the ford at Smith Shoals became impassable when the Cumberland River was high. Wagons returning to Jacksboro were usually loaded with salt from the Goose Creek works.

The point of land at the meeting of the rivers had no settlers to discuss the great events of 1812: the strongest earthquake in United States history, the War of 1812, and the first trip by steamboat, made by the *New Orleans*, from Pittsburgh to New Orleans. The New Madrid, Missouri, earthquake knocked down chimneys as far away as Cincinnati and among other changes in the landscape formed Reelfoot Lake in west Tennessee, but it left Pulaski County unharmed. Three companies of Pulaski County men with two from Wayne County fought in the War of 1812. The future site of Burnside had no men to go. The one event in 1812 important in the future history of Burnside was the trip of the *New Orleans*. The small sidewheeler demonstrated that a steamboat could navigate the Ohio and Mississippi even during an earthquake. Other steamboats were soon carrying passengers and cargoes up and down the Mississippi and her tributaries. Cumberland River was a tributary navigable for 516 miles.

William Beaty and other farmers who lived on the highland in a bend of the Cumberland above Smith Shoals, in order to get their produce to market, had to ship it from the closest accessible point below the shoals—and this meant a spot in what would be Burnside. Sometime during the early years a road of sorts—little better than a packhorse trail—was made down the hill, across the floodplain, and to the rivers. Farmers were then able to bring goods intended for shipment down the Cumberland when there was a good tide, and in turn receive merchandise from far places. Here, near the meeting of the rivers, they waited for a boat or had one built and ready.

Boatmen on the South Fork, who also knew the place that would be Burnside, preferred high but falling tides. At such times, they could sometimes be seen guiding heavily laden broadhorns and dugouts down the South Fork past the point of land and into Cumberland River to continue for 325 miles to Nashville.

Cargo coming down the South Fork, like that from the Cumberland below, consisted of farm produce, kegs of saltpeter, and, occasionally, cedar fence posts. A good many sacks of goose feathers were sold, and more barrels of lard and cured pork, but corn and tobacco were the main crops.

The justices of Pulaski County, realizing that all farm produce for sale—except horsestock, cattle, and hogs able to walk to market—would have to go down Cumberland River, in 1801 ordered two warehouses built at different points on the northern side of the river, each warehouse to have three inspectors. All hemp, flour, and tobacco intended for shipment was to be brought to a warehouse for inspection. Craft coming down the South Fork with cargoes of tobacco had to cross the Cumberland and tie off below the inspection point on Samuel Newell's land.

Pulaski County records refer to hemp, wheat, flax, barley, oats, rye, and cotton, but always in small quantities for local use. The floodplains of the rivers and the virgin soil of the uplands grew fine crops of corn and tobacco. Large quantities of tobacco as cargo were often found. In 1817, for example, the inspectors of one warehouse reported having inspected 294 hogsheads of tobacco during the shipping season. Each hogshead weighed 2,200 pounds.

Important as tobacco was, it was second to corn as a cash crop in Pulaski County. The corn, of course, had to be made into whiskey before it found a ready sale in Nashville or New Orleans. It was not uncommon to find more than a thousand gallons of whiskey "in good tight barrels" in inventories of dead men's estates. Most farmers had from one to three stills with accompanying sprouting and mash tubs. A good deal of whiskey was used locally, selling for only twenty-five to thirty cents per gallon. Comparable whiskey brought at least one dollar per gallon in Nashville.

Most boatmen walked home, but occasionally when spring was on the way, a boat rowed by strong-backed, hard-muscled men would pass the point of land on the way up the South Fork. They, like boatmen on other Mississippi tributaries, were bringing goods from Nashville or New Orleans. Now and then one of these craft would tie off on the eastern bank of the South Fork to unload cargo or wait for buyers.

Not all merchandise from the outside world came up the river. A good deal was brought by packhorse from Lexington. Judging from county records and other sources, many Pulaski countians accumulated a variety of possessions from the outside world—from leghorn bonnets and patented lanterns to Bateman's "Ague and Fever Drops." Jean, linsey, and other homemade materials were found, but more common and several times as expensive were broadcloth, silk, fine cottons and other imported materials. There was also quite a variety of books, along with quires of writing paper and the usual inkstands and ink.

We find records of sums paid for the tuition of girls and boys; the latter after some elementary education were sometimes sent to one of the several academies in the Bluegrass. Local teachers, like local ministers, worked part time for small wages; some eked out a livelihood by farming. Judging from the large number of men certified by the justices to practice law, some lawyers had lean years. They may or may not have farmed. During the 1820s and earlier, lists of dead men's debts often contain quite large doctors' bills. The several doctors who practiced in Pulaski County had at this time no formal training in medicine. There were also blacksmiths, farriers, carpenters, chair makers, boat builders, hatters, masons, tanners, wheelwrights, and others who did not live entirely by farming.

As long as the binding of children was legal, we learn of the presence of skilled workmen through binding agreements that were overseen by the court. Not all boys were sent to school, nor did all girls have "fancy shawls" and "waist ribbons." Both sexes, often fatherless, were bound at the age of twelve or younger. Boys were bound until twenty-one years of age to serve skilled workmen while learning a trade; girls had to serve until eighteen and learn housewifery. The law demanded that all bound children be treated in a "kindly" manner, given a "wholesome diet," and taught reading, writing, and arithmetic to the rule of three.

Binding agreements were signed without addresses, no doubt because, except for Clio and Somerset, the only place names were those of the creeks and rivers. Several localities slowly acquired names: the highland surrounded by a bend of the Cumberland that began at Smith Shoals became Antioch; the place where Samuel Tate had settled on the Jacksboro Road south of future Burnside became known as Tateville, the name it bears today. Sloan's Valley, several miles further south and also on the Jacksboro Road, was named for Benjamin Sloan, who had settled there before the road was built. Waitsboro, a short distance below the mouth of the South Fork, but on the northern side of the Cumberland, was named for Cyrenius Wait, from Massachusetts. He did not come until 1818, but soon became important in the business, educational, and political affairs of Pulaski County.

The empty point of land between the rivers became Point Isabel. One story goes that a lovelorn girl named Isabel leaped into the river to her death, but as no one knows the last name of this Isabel or the name of her faithless lover, the tale remains only a tale.

Yet it is true that one day early in April 1833, a small steamboat, the *Jefferson*, captained by E. S. Burge, came all the way from Nashville and tied off at Point Isabel on the eastern shore of the South Fork. The more sophisticated who had seen steamboats in Nashville were no doubt as excited as those who had never seen such a craft or heard a long-drawn steamboat whistle. The *Jefferson* stayed long enough to take on a cargo of tobacco and then returned to Nashville.

Judge Byrd Douglas in *Steamboatin' on the Cumberland* equates the feat of the *Jefferson* in navigating the uncharted Cumberland to Point Isabel with that of the *Virginia*, which in 1817 was the first steamboat to ascend the Mississippi all the way to Fort Snelling, just below Minneapolis.

One can better appreciate the courage and skill of the men who sailed the sternwheelers to Point Isabel by reading the first survey of Cumberland River, made three years after the first trip of the *Jefferson*. Sylvester Welch, chief engineer of Kentucky, supervised the work and reported to Governor Owsley; the report, included in the Kentucky *Senate Journal* of 1836–1837, is now in the archives of the Kentucky Historical Society.

Engineer Welch found Wild Goose Shoals, farther down the river, one of the worst spots. Here "a bed of rock projects into the river from the left or southern shore about 250 feet. The higher points of the rock appear to be about 18 inches above the low water plane. The deep channel which boats would follow passes to the right of and around the bed of rock and then to the left to avoid a gravel bar below."

The engineer saw these shoals and others as hazards for barges; it was not until he neared the Kentucky-Tennessee line that he mentioned some of the dangers to steamboats. Among these were the logs and snags in the channels and the fifteen islands scattered through the navigable part of the Cumberland above the Tennessee line. "The islands," Welch wrote, "generally occupy the middle of the river leaving a channel on each side from 60 to 70 or 130 to 140 feet wide. Trees grow upon the slopes of the banks along the channels and lean over the water, in some instances 40 or 50 feet, or they sometimes cover more than half the width of the channel. If the current presses the boat toward the shore the chimneys and wheelhouses are brought into contact with the leaning trees, and frequently are broken or otherwise injured." He found the remains of an old mill as a further obstruction.

Welch suggested many improvements to be made on the part of the Cumberland above the Tennessee line, but help for navigation was slow in coming. There are a few steamboatmen left who ran the Cumberland during the last years of steamboating. They remember with headshakes Wild Goose Shoals and other particularly hazardous stretches.

Equally dangerous, or perhaps worse, were the thick fogs that settled over the river on many nights. Raftsmen tied up at night, but steamboat and barge captains usually continued, no matter what the weather. During thick fogs, a pilot had only his ears for guides as he judged his craft's distance from shore by the time required for the widening furrow of the paddle wheel to lap against the shore. Barge and keelboatmen usually yelled and timed the return of the echo to get some idea of the distance to shore.

Still, when tides were sufficient, sternwheelers from Nashville managed to reach Point Isabel, where they put off and took on cargo as at other ports of call down the Cumberland. Captains of these craft soon gave Point Isabel the title "Head of Navigation of the Cumberland River," but for sixteen years after the coming of the first packet there was no settler at Point Isabel to be proud of that title.

The hundred or more men who left Pulaski County to fight in the 1846 War with Mexico had not yet returned when in 1849 a handful of Pulaski countians left by steamboat to hunt gold in California. During this same year a great event happened in Point Isabel: the first settler came.

James Ballou, fifty-one years old and of French descent, paid Daniel Smith and his wife, Elizabeth, $1,000 for a large boundary of land that began on Cumberland River and extended over most of what would become lower Burnside, excluding a strip of land along the South Fork.

James Ballou no doubt knew the Cumberland sometimes flooded wide areas of land. He built his home on higher but level land quite a distance from the rivers, where the tides

11

never came. The two-story house with wide porches for both stories was of weatherboard and frame construction and was in good condition in the Burnside I knew as a child. The lumber for the Ballou home had been cut by a fairly new invention—a rotary saw powered by steam. Such a saw could within a few minutes cut more lumber than the earlier whip or pit saw, powered by two men, a horse, or a stream of water. The rotary saw had been in use since 1830 and was not long in reaching Pulaski County. Most of the first log homes of early settlers were by 1849 being weatherboarded or replaced by frame or brick.

There were fifteen children in the Ballou home, and shortly after moving to Point Isabel, they began to marry and settle in homes of their own. One of the older Ballou boys, Levi, bought a small tract of land from his father; less than a year later he put up a dwelling and married Polly Ann Lewis. He sold out in 1857 to W. T. Heath and moved away. Another Ballou boy, Allen, married Nancy Lewis, daughter of John Shelby Lewis, and settled nearby in Antioch. Allen is one of the best remembered of James Ballou's children, partly because he lived until 1928, dying at ninety, but mainly because of the sermons many older people had heard him preach in the Antioch Church of Christ and elsewhere.

During the next several years, Point Isabel remained a sparsely settled farming community inhabited by the Ballous, Heaths, and other families named Jones and Alsop who had come later. Steamboats continued to come to Point Isabel, usually between late November and early May when heavy rainfall brought high tides to the Cumberland. The small packets, though slow by today's standards, greatly shortened the time needed to get produce to market and gave any person with the fare an opportunity to visit or do business in the wider world. A passenger could take a packet at Point Isabel, travel to Nashville, and there take a larger boat for Cincinnati, New Orleans, Pittsburgh, Saint Louis, or any other port in the Mississippi River system.

Like the keelboats before them, the sternwheelers brought rice, coffee, tea, and sugar, while a boat on the "Christmas tide" brought candy, oranges, bananas, chocolate, and other foods then considered luxuries. Most boats carried piece goods and wearing apparel. The packets also brought larger items keelboatmen had seldom, if ever, handled. Packets brought circular saws and steam engines to Point Isabel, along with farming implements, wire fencing, heating stoves, and a good deal of furniture.

Horsehair sofas, rosewood parlor tables, massive walnut or mahogany veneer wardrobes and other fashionable furniture, most of it factory made, were soon being used in several homes. The corner cupboards, Jackson presses, blanket chests and beds made of solid walnut or cherry by local craftsmen were relegated to attics or given to the help.

During my childhood there were several homes in which the housewife would say, pointing to a piece of furniture, "My granpa bought that in New Orleans, and brought it all the way to our landing by steamboat, away back before The War."

I knew which war was meant, though I had never heard anyone at home or in Burnside say "Civil War" or "War between the States"; many of the handed-down stories I heard at home began: "It was back before The War."

The custom may have come about through caution, politeness, or remembered sorrow mixed with fear and horror. Sufferings from the actual fighting were small compared to the bloody wreckage in Tennessee. There was in Pulaski County only one important battle.

Confederate General Felix Zollicoffer was killed and his troops defeated by Union forces commanded by General George H. Thomas at the Battle of Logan's Crossroads, January 19–20, 1862. The well-known battle is often referred to as the Battle of Mill Springs because General Zollicoffer and his troops encamped there for several days before crossing the Cumberland to meet the enemy.

One of the saddest effects of The War was the division among the population. Men left to fight for the Confederates; more fought for the Union. Communities, church bodies, and even homes were divided. Yet, most stories I used to hear of The War were of the guerrillas, who if they couldn't steal a horse or meat from the smokehouse would take it at gunpoint, and then set fire to the home and farm buildings.

Greatest sufferers from the guerrillas were those who lived south of the Cumberland or near the better of the two roads in southern Pulaski County; the better one went from Somerset to the crossing of the Cumberland at Waitsboro, continued southwestward through Monticello, Albany, and into Tennessee. Soldiers also passed back and forth on the road, and were always foraging to supply their needs, taking horses, food, and panels of rail fence for cooking fires.

The few settlers at Point Isabel, no different from others round about, were no longer permitted to sell farm produce at Nashville. They also had to do without sugar, coffee, rice, and everything else the steamboats had once brought; the packets had stopped coming into Kentucky, even before President Lincoln, on August 16, 1861, forbade trade with the enemy. However, this was a minor problem compared to The War and the depredations of the well-armed brigands who claimed to be guerrillas fighting for one side or the other. As war deepened, most men of military age were gone. Still, the so-called guerrillas ambushed many old men and half-grown boys who never saw their murderers.

Most of the inhabitants of Point Isabel were probably pleased by thoughts of protection when Union General Ambrose E. Burnside, in command of a good-sized body of troops, came in March 1863 to make the place his headquarters. The general, a West Point graduate, had had so far an up-and-down career. Promoted to the rank of major-general, he was sent late in 1862 to the Army of the Potomac, commanded by General George B. McClellan. President Lincoln, angered by McClellan's failure to capture General Robert E. Lee and his army, replaced McClellan with Burnside. Shortly after taking command, Burnside with 113,000 troops was defeated by Lee with 75,000 men at the Battle of Fredericksburg, December 13, 1862.

Burnside was at once replaced by General Joseph Hooker and relegated to the command of the Department of the Ohio. It was in this capacity that he came to Point Isabel, his purpose to stop Confederate troops that might enter Kentucky by the Cumberland River or the Somerset-Tennessee border road.

On reaching Point Isabel, one of Burnside's first acts was to commandeer the home of James Ballou for his headquarters. Some of the local old-timers thought Burnside did not sleep there, but spent his nights in one of the lookout homes in the highlands around Clio. Wherever the general slept, during the day he was at the house, planning work for his troops.

He fortified the hills and highlands around Point Isabel and on either side of the steamboat landing, placing more cannon and sentries above the Cumberland down to Waitsboro. Roads had to be built before cannon could be moved to the designated positions. He built a steep, twisting, but all-weather, road that connected the Somerset-Waitsboro road with the northern bank of Cumberland River opposite the mouth of the South Fork; other roads passed through and around Point Isabel. All were made of cedar logs laid side by side, each as long as the roads were wide. They lasted for generations.

Point Isabel residents and others protected by pickets and cannon were safe from the brigands. Guerrillas did little damage between Burnside and Somerset, but south of the Cumberland beyond the general's protection they picked the country clean of horses, mules, cured meat, cattle and hogs to be killed for food, and corn and wheat for human or horse fare. There was nothing left to feed the Union troops and seemingly no way of getting supplies.

In the spring of 1863, General Burnside wrote to President Lincoln, requesting authority to extend the railway from Nicholasville, Kentucky, the sixty miles or so to Somerset. A group of Cincinnati businessmen had built the railway between Ludlow, Kentucky, and Nicholasville. There was no bridge over the Ohio River to Cincinnati; the builders had planned to build the bridge and extend the line southward, but The War had stopped them.

President Lincoln gave Burnside permission to build the railway from Nicholasville to Somerset; the work could be done as a military project. General Burnside on June 23, 1863, directed W. A. Gunn of Lexington to survey the route. Gunn finished the survey and a small amount of grading was done. The work stopped; Congress had voted no funds for completion of the railway.

At long last, word of Burnside's plight reached General Grant. He ordered provisions sent to Burnside. The *Silver Cloud*, carrying supplies, with the gunboat *Reindeer* for protection, came up the Cumberland in January of 1864. The only accounts of trouble during the trip are handed-down tales of rebels hiding behind brush and rocks above the river and taking potshots at the boats. The *Reindeer* would in turn shell the spots from which the shots had sounded.

Burnside had his headquarters in Point Isabel almost a year, though he was not always there. A few times when he heard that a body of Confederates was close, he took a contingent of his men to turn back the enemy. There was one skirmish north of Somerset, but other times the only enemy found was a rumor. Burnside left with all his troops in the early spring of 1864 and reached Virginia in time to take part in the Battle of the Wilderness, May 5–6, 1864.

POINT ISABEL
BECOMES BURNSIDE

THE END OF THE WAR did not automatically bring happiness to all the people of Pulaski County. Some were angered over the loss of their slaves; many blacks were doing the same work they had done as slaves but were now being paid. Those for the Confederacy felt the sorrow of defeat, while most grieved for the dead Lincoln. Many men who had gone to war did not come home. They were dead. Many of those who returned were blind or had lost an arm or leg. Others were in poor health from battlefield hardships or time spent as prisoners of war.

Some veterans south of the Cumberland returned to impoverished farms and the graves of friends and relatives killed by guerrillas. They often found mistrust and hatred among neighbors and relatives where there had been friendship and love. In some communities in southern Pulaski and Wayne counties churches continued with only women in their congregations; men of different political opinions refused to worship together. Worse than open disagreements were the suspicions and never-proven allegations that so-and-so had bushwhacked a relative or that a certain family had fed and housed guerrillas.

There were pleasanter things new to returning soldiers; one of these was a product too thick for syrup and too thin to be called a solid, sweet with a peculiar sweetness, and in color a few shades lighter than dark-fired tobacco. The stuff was known as sorghum molasses. It was made from the juice of a variety of sorghum cane introduced into the United States in 1850. Pulaski countians showed little interest in the tall grasslike plant with sweet juice until The War stopped the importation of sugar. Farmers learned how to get the juice from the stalks and evaporate it by boiling until the once-thin juice was thick. Many families developed such a taste for sorghum molasses that they continued to use it after sugar returned to the countryside.

Point Isabel was the only place south of the Cumberland that had profited from The War. Her few inhabitants had no more money—perhaps less—but there were roads where none had been before. A ferry across the Cumberland River now connected Point Isabel with Burnside's new road that twisted its way up the steep hill on the northern side of the Cumberland and soon reached the road to Somerset.

People living near Cumberland River no doubt felt good times were back when they heard the musical notes of a steamboat whistle. The packet came on the late fall tides of 1866, and after stopping at ports along the way, tied off at the usual place on the eastern side of the South Fork.

Point Isabel already had a new settler, William Lewis. Earlier in 1866, he had bought land from W. T. Heath and was having a home built. A few months later, the small place had its first business—a retail store owned by Joe Ballou. Mrs. Baker Grissom, Sr., of Burnside, showed me a photograph of this store, at that time the only building on the point of land between the rivers.

Many in Somerset and Point Isabel already knew that immediately after The War, the same group of Cincinnati men who had built the Ludlow-Nicholasville railroad were making plans. Their railway would begin in Cincinnati, hook up with the line at Ludlow by means of an Ohio River bridge, and then continue from Nicholasville all the way to Chattanooga. The line was to be known as the Cincinnati Southern Railway.

At last in 1872 the necessary federal and state permissions

were secured, and W. A. Gunn—the same who had surveyed for General Burnside—finished surveying the route to Chattanooga. Railway buyers were soon in and above Point Isabel, buying a wide strip of land high on the hillside above the Cumberland for the right-of-way, more land near the road to Antioch for a passenger station, and, on the other side of the road, a larger boundary of high rolling land. Here a hotel and restaurant to serve railway passengers would be built. Later, during 1874–1875, the railway bought from James Ballou four small tracts near the South Fork. Here the freight depot would be built near the steamboat landing.

The first contracts were let in December 1873. There were several, including one for the construction of the Cumberland River bridge, another for the railway above Point Isabel, and still another for two tunnels, totaling 2,232 feet, on the northern side of the river. The southernmost of the two opened on the bridge a short distance upriver from Point Isabel and so high above the Cumberland there was no danger from floods. This bridge crossed the river at an angle of four degrees in order to reach a specified point high on the steep, rocky hillside south of the river. Here the route had to be blasted and dug out of rock all the way to the passenger station. A few hundred feet past the station and the road crossing, the tracks crossed a low creek valley. A giant causeway had to be built, with a cement-walled tunnel in the bottom of the fill to let the creek water through.

Grading, which grew more difficult as the line went southward into higher hills, was done by man, horse and mule power, and dynamite. Convicts did most of the pick-and-shovel work. Bulldozers, draglines, and other fuel-powered machines were not yet in use.

In 1874, before the railway had finished buying land, Point Isabel had her first realtor—Joseph Kinsey of Cincinnati. He paid the Ballous, who had already sold several lots, $9,000 for the remainder of their land. The Ballous left Point Isabel, most of them settling in Antioch. Meanwhile, Mr. Kinsey returned home and gave the land to his son-in-law, C. W. Cole, who formed a land company and divided the Ballou land into lots for sale. Cole remained active in local affairs until his death in 1905. The land company he formed is still in existence.

The right-of-way was, by the time Mr. Cole had established his business, ready for ties and rails. Carpenters and masons had come to build the passenger and freight stations. J. K. Lawrence came as a contractor for the railway hotel, Point Isabel's first. This was the town's finest structure, a three-story, thirty-two room brick building with a stone basement.

Other buildings in Point Isabel and the two stations were of frame construction. The lumber and most of the ties for the railway were furnished by three small companies—Buffalo Tie, Archer-Mancourt, and Rhodes Junk Lumber—which began operations by the rivers around 1877.

Most of the material for the railway not produced in Point Isabel was brought by steamboat. *Skipper's Own*, captained by Tom Ryan, brought the span for the Cumberland River bridge. Supplies may have come by wagon from Somerset after the railway reached that place, on July 23, 1877; the Ohio River bridge was finished in December 1877.

The first train, a passenger on its way to Chattanooga, passed through Point Isabel, February 21, 1880. Trustees of the Cincinnati Southern leased their line to the Cincinnati, New Orleans & Texas Pacific Railway in 1881, and the railway was known as the C.N.O. & T.P. This name was changed back to Cincinnati Southern when in 1894 that company gained control of the C.N.O. & T.P.

The opening of the railway not only meant easier and quicker transportation for goods and people to and from Point Isabel but also mail service. The twice-weekly mail route from Somerset to the Tennessee line, established in 1848, had bypassed Point Isabel and crossed the Cumberland River at Waitsboro. The Jacksboro Road route served the Sloans, Tates, and others but not the people of Point Isabel. We don't know how many local residents had been walking or riding back and forth to Somerset for mail, but we do know of one. Young George P. Taylor, a native of Maine who had come in 1878, walked daily over the unfinished railway to the Somerset post office until 1880. A Point Isabel post office was established that year. Taylor was first a co-owner of a retail store; when this store burned a few years later, he established a produce house with a branch in Somerset; next he formed the Cumberland Grocery Company, a wholesale house. He was soon one of Pulaski County's leading businessmen.

Point Isabel continued to grow. Two years after the railway was completed, one of the few licensed physicians in the county, Dr. Littleton Cook, began practicing in the town. He also owned the first drugstore, opened in 1884. Young Nicholas D. Stigall of Pulaski County clerked in the store for several years for $6.25 per month, and board, before going to Louisville Medical School. He returned as an M.D. in 1901 to spend the next forty-seven years as the locality's best-loved and busiest physician.

Others who came to stay during the 1880s include J. L. Grissom, who owned the drugstore for a time and was active in other businesses; John W. Sloan, born in Pulaski County, who spent more than fifty years in the town, and Colonel R. M. Phillippi, a four-year veteran of the 11th Pennsylvania Infantry, who came in 1880 as superintendent of Archer, Mancourt & Company. In 1884, the largest lumber company yet to come to Point Isabel, Kentucky Lumber, bought and enlarged Archer, Mancourt. Kentucky Lumber needed a good many workers and to house them had a large building erected on the hill above the railway station, only one of several buildings rising above and below the railway tracks.

A. C. French came from New Hampshire in 1886 to establish another lumber company. It handled only cedar: faucets, most of which were shipped to the wineries of Europe; fence posts; cedar lumber; and later the wooden parts of pencils.

Point Isabel had gained in importance when in 1884 the Somerset-Monticello stagecoach and mail route stopped going by way of Waitsboro and came to Point Isabel. Here the stagecoach met the passenger trains. The so-called Burnside-Monticello Pike had stretches of axle-deep mud during wet weather, while Bronston Hill with its steep hairpin curves and rock ledges was a nightmare in all weathers for mules pulling loaded wagons up and for stagecoach passengers coming down at a swift pace in order to meet the morning passenger train. All—from the stagecoach to the goose walking to market—had to pay toll.

Save for the war years, packets had been coming and going from Point Isabel for about half a century. Yet during this time no one in Point Isabel had owned or built a packet. This changed when A. B. Massey, who came in 1886, set up a boatyard suitable for building packets. The first Massey sternwheeler, the *Crescent*, went off the ways during the spring tide of 1888. Massey was soon known as Captain Massey.

Point Isabel, now with several hundred people, was incorporated in 1890 and renamed Burnside in honor of General Burnside. A mayor, town clerk, and marshal were chosen, a police court organized, a jail built, and taxes levied for the upkeep of the town and school. The place had an elementary school, Sunday school, and a Presbyterian church. The church was built of stone in 1885 near the former home of James Ballou. The town also had retail stores, saloons, a post office, ferries across both rivers, and hotels.

Yearly, more railway passengers, freight, and mail were coming and going through Burnside to and from Wayne, Cumberland, and other counties with no railway. There were several restaurants in town, some for workers but most for travelers. The largest, grandest, and longest-lasting hotel, the Seven Gables, was built during the nineties. One of the earliest was the Burnside Hotel.

The name *Burnside* began to appear in the titles of other businesses. French named his business the Burnside Manufacturing Company, though most Burnsiders continued to call it "the cedar mill." Captain Massey named his second packet *Burnside No. 1*. Soon he, his son Kenneth, Captain Dave Heath, and two other men organized the Burnside & Burkesville Transportation Company, known on many rivers as the B. & B. line. The company prospered, built and bought more packets, and in time owned fifteen barges. Few of the B. & B. boats went to Nashville; mostly they, like the others that came to Burnside, worked the ninety-mile stretch of the

Cumberland between Burnside and Burkesville, where cargoes were transferred to or from larger craft. The *Albany*, a B. & B. packet built at Burnside in 1901, was an exception. Different from other Burnside packets, she carried cargo to and from Nashville, and like many other packets strong enough for the business, she often served as a towboat.

Railway competition made packets less important to life in Burnside than they had once been, though the federal government had somewhat improved navigation. The first United States district engineer had come to Nashville in 1873; within a few years the engineers were able to maintain a few work boats that kept the Cumberland free of floating trees and similar hazards, but had not yet built locks and dams; the shoals, tricky passages around islands, and fog all remained as hazards.

Byrd Douglas after much research was able to write in *Steamboatin' on the Cumberland* that during the early nineties trade from the stretch of the river between Burkesville and Point Isabel was still worth ten million dollars yearly in Nashville. During 1895, for example, Kentucky cargo that reached Nashville from the upper Cumberland consisted of: "10,000,000 feet of hardwood lumber; 200,000 minimum of crossties; a large quantity of ax handles and staves; 3,200 hogsheads of tobacco; 100,000 pounds of cured meat and lard; 3,500 head of livestock; 30,000 head of hogs; 30,000 tons of grain and hay; 150,000 full coops of chickens, turkeys, and ducks; 100,000 cases of eggs; 60,000 gallons of sorghum molasses; and several thousand tons of hides, furs, walnuts, and wild herbs." Much of this had been carried as far as Burkesville by the B. & B. line.

Cargoes were changing, and the biggest change was the continual lessening of goods shipped by steamboat. Cattle and hogs driven to the Burnside stockyards had once waited for the coming of a steamboat; now they waited a much shorter time to be driven up to cattle cars on the railway siding. Farmers and their wives downriver who shipped poultry to Nashville would soon be bringing or shipping it to George P. Taylor Produce in Burnside.

Shortly after establishing his produce house, Taylor gave "settings" of Plymouth Rock eggs to each of his customers. He did this to improve the chickens he handled. The Barred Plymouth Rock or "Dominecker" was the best general-purpose breed then known.

Taylor sold a variety of feeds for domestic animals and dealt in hides, dried herbs, and other produce from the back hills, but his biggest business was shipping eggs and freshly killed and cleaned chickens packed in ice to Chattanooga, Cincinnati, and New York. In order to have a regular supply of ice, he installed an ice manufacturing plant, big enough for his needs and those of Burnside. A horse-drawn, water-dripping wagon with the driver yelling "ice" was soon making daily rounds in Burnside.

The manufacture of ice would have been difficult before the Burnside Water Company was formed by Cole, French, Geary, and Captain Massey. This company was soon able to supply Burnside homes and businesses with running water, properly purified. The wells and springs that had formerly supplied water fell into disuse, as did the privies at the back of each lot.

Meanwhile the hotel built by the railway was of no use to its owners. Railway passengers ate in dining cars and slept in Pullman cars. C. W. Cole acquired the building and offered the free use of it for educational purposes. Dr. E. H. Pearce, president of Kentucky Wesleyan College, with the help of Dr. Stigall and other Burnsiders, founded Kentucky Wesleyan Academy and housed it in the railway hotel. The first students came in the autumn of 1897. Locally known as the Burnside Academy, this school was the first Wesleyan preparatory school in the state.

The curriculum, much like that of other preparatory schools of that time, ranged from geology and natural philosophy to trigonometry and Greek. There was plenty of space in the former hotel for classes, living quarters for teachers and boarding students, and cooking and dining facilities. The school also accepted day pupils; among these were several Burnside boys.

There were many boys in Burnside by 1900, when the

town's population had grown to two thousand. The fathers and often the sons worked at a variety of jobs: they were masons and house carpenters, boatyard carpenters and mechanics, shop and hotel keepers, blacksmiths, ferrymen, managers and owners of businesses, teachers, railway clerks, section hands, agents, butchers, saloon keepers—and captains, pilots, clerks, cooks, and deckhands on the steamboats. Yet all of these together were not so numerous as the millhands. The timber coming down the rivers was the basis of Burnside's being. Men far up the river were cutting timber or hewing crossties for the Burnside mills.

The timber around Burnside became better known when a giant piece was shipped from Somerset. The length of poplar, so long three flatcars were needed to transport it, won first place at the Chicago World's Fair in 1893. The tree from which it came had grown in Pumpkin Hollow across Cumberland River from the beginning of Antioch Bend.

Practically all timber produced in Burnside was shipped by rail as was most of the incoming steamboat cargo. All this freight had to be loaded onto mule-drawn vehicles, hauled up the hill, and reloaded into cars on the siding. This slow and tedious procedure ended in 1894 when C. W. Cole and B. Q. Gasner formed the Burnside & Cumberland River Railway. This was a beltline that came down from the railway siding in a long and fairly gentle southward slope below the main line, then turned in a wide curve that, with another curve, took it to the freight depot in the lower town. Along the way switch lines were built into the loading yards. Lumber was loaded directly into waiting cars and hauled up to the main line by Number Five engine, known in Burnside as the switch line engine.

Burnside's first and only bank was organized in 1900 by twelve local businessmen, who erected a brick and cement building low in the town near Kentucky Lumber. The following year, the largest lumber company yet, Chicago Veneer, bought and greatly enlarged Rhodes Junk Lumber Company. The main job of the new company was to cut poplar veneer for the Pullman Company near Chicago, but it also shipped large quantities of hardwood lumber. A new business as always meant new people in Burnside, among them were the managers: B. W. Lord and S. J. Glanton.

The people of Burnside, who had once looked to Nashville and the deeper South for markets, news, and supplies, were turning slowly but surely toward the North. Trains carried their timber and farm produce to markets in northern cities. There were weekly newspapers in Somerset, but more and more Burnsiders were reading dailies published in Cincinnati or Lexington, and usually a Louisville Sunday paper. Northern and eastern manufacturers had begun to look to Burnside for the hardwood they needed.

However, not all Burnsiders had turned northward. The *Burnside No. 2*, *Albany*, *City of Burkesville*, *Celina No. 2*, *Crescent*, *Creelsboro*, *Rowena*—all B. & B. line packets—continued to carry cargo, although in smaller quantities. In 1904, the switch line was extended down to a floating dock making it possible to transfer cargo directly between packet and freight cars. Packet passengers were also accommodated; P. W. Tuttle, the passenger agent, could sell tickets to any railway station in the United States.

The B. & B. line now had to compete with another Burnside packet company—the Cumberland Transportation Company, organized by George P. Taylor and his son, Norman. Tom Lewis was general manager. Their first boats were gasoline launches, but the company soon turned to sternwheelers: the *W. G. Nixon*, *Patrol*, and *City of Nashville*. Both companies were noted for their courageous and skillful captains: Massey, Dave Heath, and his three sons, Clate, John, and Otho for the B. & B. Line; B. L. Ham, Frank Campbell, and Bridges Montgomery for the other company.

Modernizations came swiftly; the railway had brought Burnside a telegraph line; the first telephone directory was issued in 1903. Shortly afterward the town voted a bond issue for the building of a public graded and high school. Burnside Wesleyan Academy had ended its work in Burnside. The red brick building that housed Burnside Graded and High School soon stood high on the road that led up the hill past the passenger station. A board of trustees was elected. The town was proud of the building and of having a nine-month school. A state-wide public school system was slow in reaching Kentucky, and high schools continued scarce, several counties having none at all.

A short distance down the hill from the school, the Methodists built their handsome brick church in 1907. The brick and concrete Masonic Temple was built in 1911 just above the Methodist Church. Several years after the local Freemason Lodge was founded in the 1880s (then with no building of its own), wives and daughters of the members organized a local chapter of the Order of the Eastern Star, named Grace Lawrence Chapter in honor of Dr. Stigall's wife, daughter of Patti Beaty and J. K. Lawrence. Older than the Methodist Church and the Masonic Temple was the Baptist Church, built on the opposite side of the upper town in 1900–1901.

These buildings and many others in the town were soon lighted by electricity, though Burnside's early electric lights were sometimes less bright than the kerosine lamps they displaced. John W. Sloan had bought the Burnside Water Company in 1907. Later, he installed an electric generator powered by steam.

According to Lindley Mitchell, who had in 1912 settled near Burnside with his parents and younger sister, Bernice: "When the steam was low or the belt slipping, the filament would become a dull red. Occasionally the belt would break and we would be without lights until the belt was replaced." He also remembered the street lights that were "no more than about four feet high with a reflector and a regular light bulb, maybe 100 to 150 watts."

Life in Burnside was not all school and work. There had always been the usual pastimes of the day with the rivers affording more—for men only in the early years. The first organized sport was baseball, which appears to have begun as soon as there were enough men and boys able to play. The games continued—in spite of the angry condemnation by several members of one church—until the playing field up the road past the Seven Gables went under Lake Cumberland.

27

Nobody objected to baseball as such, but the only time Burnside players and those of opposing teams could get together was on Sunday, when those who worked were free. To some the playing of any game on Sunday was breaking the Fourth Commandment.

Love of music came with the first Burnsiders. Among the several music makers, the greatest was J. L. Grissom, who played several instruments. In 1908 he organized a band. Grissom's son, Baker, only ten years old, played the cornet. The two Grissoms, Lonnie Bryant, and several others, playing only for pleasure, first held practice sessions in the Grissom home; as the band grew larger, members met in an empty store. Glory was added to pleasure when at the Pulaski County Fair the Burnside Band played in competition with Somerset and won.

Burnside has the distinction of having had the first Boy Scout troop in the United States, but during the troop's five-year existence it was never a member of the national organization, and thus the claim has no official standing. While visiting in England in 1908, Mrs. William Bass became interested in the Boy Scouts, recently founded by Lord Baden-Powell. On her return to Burnside, Mrs. Bass brought a copy of the official handbook, *Scouting for Boys*, just published in England. She at once set about organizing fifteen boys into a troop. They chose the name Eagle Troop, but the handbook stipulated the leader must be a man. The organizer's husband, William Bass, became leader while Mrs. Bass continued as director.

Mr. Bass, an all-around athlete, introduced a game new to the boys—basketball. The boys liked the game so well that when Eagle Troop at last had five dollars in the treasury, they voted to disband and spend their five dollars for a basketball. Burnside had no other troop of Scouts for several years, but basketball was there to stay.

A boy with a bit of time on his hands could watch the building of the South Fork River bridge, finished in 1912. The Burnside-Monticello Pike was no longer a toll road, but all using the new steel bridge had to pay toll.

One man, then living in Bronston, who during the autumn of 1912 crossed the bridge twice daily on his way to and from work was Elias Thomas Simpson. His Burnside job was "feeding the hog" at Chicago Veneer.

He had for eight years been a teacher in the Wayne County Schools and then worked for several years as a tool dresser in the Wayne County oil fields. In 1905 he had married Mollie Jane Denney, who had by 1912 borne him three daughters. He was the sole support of his wife and family, except for a share of the oil royalties from his father's land. The oil fields in Wayne County were drilled out, though still producing; thus, he came to the veneer mill.

I know, because I was the second of Elias Thomas Simpson's daughters. Our mother at last made up her mind to move to Burnside. We moved in March of 1913 while the lower town was still damp from a great flood.

3

LIFE IN LOWER BURNSIDE

I REMEMBER NOTHING of our move from Bronston to Burnside in March of 1913 when I was almost five years old; sister Elizabeth was seven, while Margaret, whom we called Peggy, was not yet two. Our new home was low in the town near where the main road reached the foot of the hill and turned left toward the South Fork.

Early mornings while still in bed, my first awareness was of darkness and sounds: almost constant, seemingly unchanging, was the clomp, clomp of mule and horse shoes in the road and the rattle and creak of wagons; long blasts from the several mill whistles, not blowing time-to-get-to-work but only time-to-be-thinking-about-getting-to-work whistles, momentarily drowned the other noises, but soon I could again hear the clomp, clomp interrupted by sounds of breakfast getting, or from the main road the clink of a cowbell; then from somewhere up the Cumberland would come a long-drawn whistle and a roar drowning out all other sounds—a freight was coming out of the tunnel and onto the bridge. The roar increased as the train ran high above and back from our house, then whistled again for the road crossing, and with a lessening roar went southward. Quite often a freight would slow, and above the diminished roaring, I could hear the train bell ring; I knew the train was going to the siding where it would either hook on freight cars waiting there or leave loaded cars or empties or both. I had heard that more freight was handled at Burnside than at any other town on the Southern Railway between Cincinnati and Chattanooga. Northbound trains made plenty of racket, but not the bone-quivering roar of most southbound freights; these were usually double-headers with the second locomotive hooked on at the Ferguson Railway Shops and roundhouse a short distance south of Somerset. Two engines were needed for the long pull up and through the mountains between us and Chattanooga.

I never lay abed listening very long before our mother was calling me from the foot of the stairs. Nightgown peeled off, other clothing on, shoes untied, face and hands dabbed in water, and brush run through my hair, I ran downstairs. My chief interest was in getting at least a hug from Papa before he left to "feed the hog" at Chicago Veneer. He worked at this job—I think "the hog" was a big fuel chute to the boiler room —except when he kept tally for several months during the next five years. The work kept him busy ten hours for six days each week. I never thought of his getting tired, but took his strength for granted. He was six feet tall with wide shoulders, but was somewhat thin, even his face. His eyes were blue, but a different blue from our mother's. I never saw much of him on workday mornings.

There were usually a few other men eating—how many I don't know; perhaps there were only two or three or even one. Our mother was trying to run a boardinghouse. The most I remember about the boarding business is the young woman who cooked and cleaned. She was kind, never "nervous" as our mother was, and would let me hang around the kitchen. I enjoyed watching her make pies; she pricked pictures into the top crust: an apple for an apple pie, a peach for peach pie, and so forth.

Pie making came later in the day. My first watching was through the dining room windows that faced the lower end of the uphill road. Here I could see Papa cross the road on his way to the mill that stretched across the lowland almost to the bank of the South Fork. Usually Papa was swallowed in the foggy dark by the time he had crossed the road. From this window I could also see the last part of the downhill road, but not the place where it turned toward the rivers.

Papa gone, there was little else to see so early in the morning. I could make out the dim yellow blur of a streetlight at the corner and the paler blurs of lanterns, bobbing along as they were carried by indistinct shapes on their way to work. I could see nothing on several early mornings when fog hung thick curtains over the windows. Our father would shake his head and hope the steamboats on the Cumberland were safe.

The time-to-work whistles blew and what I thought of as the song-of-the-saws began. I never called the sounds by that name; our mother complained of the "racket" that reached us from both the veneer mill on the other side of the uphill road and Kentucky Lumber on the Cumberland side of the road to the rivers.

The boarders, when we had any, soon left the dining room and that meant the part of the day I disliked would soon begin—sister Elizabeth's getting ready and leaving for school. She was sobbing before Mama had finished braiding her curly hair. She had been attending rural schools since she was four or five years old and at seven was in the fourth grade, but Burnside was her first graded school, and she was a stranger to her classmates and teacher.

Our mother, whom I later heard described as a "high-strung, weakly, nervous woman," had no patience with Elizabeth's tears or with any child who didn't want to go to school. She had before marriage taught ten terms of school in Wayne County, and one of the reasons for moving to Burnside was the graded and high school—and now she had a child who didn't want to go.

I couldn't blame Elizabeth for crying when Mama yanked the tangles out of her curly hair. I knew that hurt. I don't think she cried because she disliked school work. I didn't remember her crying when she had gone to Bronston school. I think she cried in Burnside because everything about the school was strange to her from its size to her teacher and classmates. She didn't seem to know the name of even one classmate.

The fog had usually thinned enough by the time I watched Elizabeth disappear up the sidewalk that I could see much of the lower town, though I do not remember the names and owners of all the buildings. There were so many, little vacant space was left in the lowland.

As the fog lifted and more daylight poured into the valley, people on foot and wagons passing by took on shape and size. My window watching was often interrupted by the remembrance of my job—care of sister Peggy when my mother and the woman who helped were busy elsewhere. It seemed to me the proper care of sister Peggy would be to tie her down. I would hear a frightened cry and look around to see her trying to climb from the arm of a chair onto the dining table with the chair tipping and one of her feet flailing the air. I would get her safely back to the floor. Confidence restored, she was ready to try again. She usually was standing in the center of the dining table before I noticed, but was never able to make it to the top of the cupboard.

Peggy watching never lasted all day. During much of the time I was free to play with my dolls and other toys, but with Burnside just beyond the windows, I preferred window watching during the dank cold days when I was not permitted outdoors.

An automobile was a rare sight. Several Burnside families owned Overlands and other makes, but almost everybody walked to work or on errands, especially to the post office (mail was not delivered in Burnside). Wagons and buggies often passed, with now and then a farm wagon carrying milk cans of cream. The cream was on its way to the express station for shipment to a cheese or butter manufacturer. Many farm wives with dairy cows took the cream out of the milk by running fresh milk through a hand-powered cream separator.

I often wished I could see inside the big mule-drawn covered wagons that came down the hill and turned onto the road to the rivers. I soon learned from Papa that the covered wagons carried groceries and other supplies from the Cumberland Grocery, Wholesalers, to stores in Wayne County with no railroad and far from a steamboat landing.

One of the most curious outfits I saw was neither buggy nor wagon, but more like a huge churn laid lengthwise on wheels, with big words on one side. It was pulled by the biggest and strongest-looking horse I had ever seen; the hair on his fetlocks hung down to his hooves. I learned from Papa he was a workhorse, a Clydesdale. He pulled a tank wagon filled with kerosine, and the words I couldn't read were STANDARD OIL.

I sometimes went to a front window in order to see H. C. Burton's sixteen-passenger motor coach stop at the post office shortly before ten o'clock each morning. The coach carried mail and passengers between Monticello and Burnside. It stayed only long enough at the post office to take on more bags of mail; then it went up to the passenger station, reaching it in time to meet the northbound local. The coach then waited for the southbound train that came a short time later.

The motor coach was a great sight, but I was less impressed by it than by the steam threshing machine I had seen snorting its way along a road in Bronston.

Mr. Burton's stagecoach was the grandest sight of all, with the driver on his high seat, cracking his long whip now and then but not touching one of the four horses, all ashine like the coach itself; there were passengers on top, more passengers inside, and mail bags swinging from the back. I saw the stagecoach going up and down the hill road, and I usually reached a front window in time to see it stop at the post office each afternoon. The outfit left Monticello at noon, and covered the twenty-one miles to Burnside in four hours including time out to change horses at a livery stable midway between the towns. The stagecoach always reached Burnside in time for the afternoon passenger trains.

The cold drizzle of late winter gave way to a warm steady rain that swelled buds and caused our mother to get busy on spring sewing. The rain worried our father. A late winter flood, he reminded us, had held up our moving; the Cumberland was still at high tide, and with more rain, he feared there'd be another flood. A second or even a third flood in a winter and a spring was not uncommon.

Papa explained to me why lower Burnside had so many

floods. It stood on a floodplain only fifty feet or less above the Cumberland at pool stage, while tides of fifty-five or sixty feet or higher were common. The South Fork did her share too in helping flood the town. I hoped for a flood; going around in skiffs and living upstairs would be fun, as well as exciting. I later learned that even a small flood brought hard work, worry, and hardship to many.

Lindley Mitchell remembers years when lower Burnside had "as many as three floods or maybe more. After the word came by telegraph from Williamsburg and New River [Tennessee] of the amount of rainfall, and the gauge at the Massey line was read, the exact height of the flood was the subject of the day. Those that would be affected (everyone from the Veneer Mill down) started to prepare by taking material off the floor and putting it on the top shelves and moving things from bottom shelves to higher ones.

"They never moved stuff any higher than their calculations of the flood, and if the water came higher than expected we waded around by lamp light, sometimes waist deep in water, putting material on the shelves still higher. . . . stacks of lumber had to be contained by Kentucky Lumber in case they floated up and turned over. Logs normally caught in the booms were sometimes swept by the 'head works.' "

The rain stopped after two or three days. The Cumberland and the South Fork ran swift and wild, lapping at the tops of their banks, but came no higher. April wind chased away the morning fogs, and we could see the sun had risen. We did not learn this from looking eastward; the East was hidden somewhere behind the hill above us. We looked westward to see a band of morning sunlight spilling over the crest of Bronston Hill. We could soon see another band of light high on the eastern-facing side of Bunker Hill, and as the sun climbed the sky, light poured onto the topmost layer of stone in the river bluff across the way. The shadow of our hill gradually moved down the bluff, crossing the Cumberland, and at last the lower town was filled with sunlight.

In using the words *east* and *west* I don't want to give the impression that Burnsiders ordinarily used points of the compass in describing the location of a home or business. Depending on where one happened to be in the town, most places in Burnside were *up* or *down*—sometimes *down* and *around*. These were the only sensible directions; the Cumberland in flowing around Burnside flowed in different directions at different points, which meant the town could never be a neat square with streets that ran north and south or east and west.

The town had streets but these had to follow the contours of the land. Robert F. Taylor, son of Norman I. Taylor, lent me a map of Burnside as it was projected in 1903. The streets— almost everybody called them roads—were given names. I seldom heard anyone use a street name. Burnside was a place where everybody knew where every other body lived and where the stores and businesses were.

Wind and sun together dried and warmed our world, and for the first time since we had moved to Burnside, Mama said I could go play on the hill directly behind the house. The hill was almost within touching distance of the back windows; looking out, I could see a square of earth so steep that I wondered how the length of tree trunk I could also see was able to stand straight and keep its footing.

The pleasures of my small outing began when the front door had closed behind me. The air was filled with the smells of freshly cut wood and of woodsmoke. The saws in the Burnside lumber mills were powered by steam, their boilers fired with scrap wood; coal was used only when the scrap ran low. Most Burnside families also heated their homes and cooked with scrap wood.

Our mother often spoke of the ugliness of lower Burnside in winter with only leafless trees to relieve the straight lines of the buildings, and everything gray-seeming under the gray sky. Yet as I stood on the front steps, low in the town, I saw no ugliness. The best sights were almost directly in front of me. Looking a bit leftward and across the road I could see first Kelsey's drugstore at the end of the sidewalk; next to it was Burnside post office, one of the grandest buildings in town with great white columns along the front. Back of and above the post office, and seeming close in spite of other buildings

36

and the 400-foot-wide Cumberland between, the high lime-stone bluff rose above the opposite side of the river. It was made of layers of limestone, some pale gray, others almost white. Smoke never seemed to dull the wall; on the grayest days it stood above the river and the town, pale and clean and beautiful.

Turning left, I could see beyond the South Fork, and on to Bronston Hill where I could make out trees, their trunks and leafless tops black against the pale rocks around and above them. Closer and further left, I could see the end of Bunker Hill rising high and steeply above the lower town, the most of it made up of layers of rocks until the top layer where I could see sloping earth and brush and trees and the rolling fields on top.

I tore myself from looking, went down the steps and around to the back of the house to begin my climb. I had planned to climb up to the railway which I knew was somewhere high on the hill. I was stopped by a high limestone ledge offering no handholds. Walking sidehill to find a place I could climb, I stopped to look down and out. I saw the Cumberland upriver from the town, but no water; the river was covered with logs—more logs than I had thought were in the world.

Looking down the Cumberland, I could see Burnside Bank, the stockyards, the machine shop, and Kentucky Lumber, but nothing of the veneer mill and other buildings farther from the river. The hill above Burnside curved away to leave a wide lowland by the rivers, but the curve ended at our house where the hillside I was on had turned up the Cumberland to leave less space between it and the river. The downhill road turned in the opposite direction. I couldn't see around the curve in the hill.

I could see the far side of the Cumberland River ferry with the ferryboat waiting on the northern shore. Here there were no logs to hide the river which was high on her banks, yellow and flecked with foam. I could see the circles of eddies and darker swirls of South Fork water not yet completely lost in the Cumberland. I wished I could see the *Rowena* or *Albany* coming up the river, but it was empty, and the South Fork after flowing out from behind Bunker Hill was still hidden by high banks and buildings.

I watched pale smoke spiral up from the tall stacks of Kentucky Lumber and saw mountains of logs, smaller piles of lumber, and men in the lumberyards. I had just seen the switch engine pulling several flatcars toward the lumberyard when from down below I heard Mama's call. She sounded worried and angry. I could see her, but she wasn't looking in my direction. The switch engine was coming on. I wanted to watch the loading of the lumber. She called again. I answered and soon learned I had been gone too long and wandered too far; I should play in a place she could see from the back windows.

Next day, I stayed on the hill within sight of the back windows. It was pure misery. I could see nothing. Mama never changed her orders about staying low on the hill, but she did let me go to the post office across the road.

The level road across lower Burnside became the main road only after the road from upper Burnside turned into it, but the crossroad continued as a seldom-used strip of bare earth upriver toward the railway bridge. Mama insisted that when going to the post office I cross this road, just above where the downhill road turned into it. There were no businesses and only a home or two past Kelsey's drugstore. I would thus be safe from speeding wagons and hard-riding "young blades." I crossed at the designated spot, though I wanted to reach the post office by running "catty-cornered" across the curve in the main road.

I enjoyed the short trip; first, I could look up into the two trees, one on either side of the strip of sidewalk that led from the street to the post office steps. Their leaves were beginning to burst out of the buds, but they were different from the leaves on other trees I saw on the hill and elsewhere. Finished with the trees, I stopped again on the top step of the post office and turned around to look at the hill above our house. I had never been able to see its top, or a train going by.

There were usually two or three people getting mail from their boxes or doing business with the postmaster behind the windows, and though all were strange to me, they gave me smiles and now and then helped me at the window, so high I had to stand on tiptoe to tell what I wanted.

A trip to the post office lost its excitement after I began to be sent to a drugstore across the street or more often to a small grocery on the same side of the street as the post office but further away. I remember little of that store, but I do remember that the errand gave me a chance to run down the street, turn toward the Cumberland River, and soon reach the Burnside Bank. There I would stand outside on the porchlike entrance above a flight of steps and look over the town and the river.

The Cumberland was high enough to let me see a stretch of it below the mouth of the South Fork. On such trips I waited, watching the river, and hoping for a steamboat, until, certain Mama would come hunting me, I ran all the way home. I had crossed the South Fork more than once on the new steel bridge, but had never seen it turn to let a steamboat pass, a sight I wanted as much as that of a steamboat coming.

I continued to watch from the porch of the Burnside Bank from which I one day saw the ferryboat, loaded with mule-drawn wagons, cross the Cumberland. Even more interesting was looking upriver to see what was going on at Kentucky Lumber. Several times I watched a tall iron giant with two long arms swing out an arm, and with the help of ropes and claws, pick a log up from the river above the boom, then turn to lay it with other logs in a pile. The two men with it looked to be doing nothing except now and then one or the other would pull on a rope. Papa told me that such log-lifters were known as derrick-cranes, but most people called them hoists or cranes.

Yet, for all my watching, I never saw the South Fork bridge turn to let a steamboat pass.

It galled me that I was never permitted to go alone up the street to Sloan & Cheely, Oakford Nunn, and other stores where our mother bought most of our groceries, clothing, sewing needs, and other dry goods. Sometimes on Saturdays I was sent on an errand with Elizabeth, but she always hurried me along and kept me so close I never had a chance to look around.

The best trips up the street were on Sundays when the whole family went to church. Members of the Christian Church to which our parents belonged as yet had no building in Burnside and worshiped in the upstairs of Oakford Nunn's store. I, in order to look my fill, tagged behind. Papa carried Peggy while Mama carried a Bible.

There was no sidewalk on our side of the uphill road which we crossed to reach the sidewalk on the other side. The uphill road rose gradually but soon it steepened. The road had been cut out of the hillside; there was, past the place where we lived, no room for a building between the road and the hill; only a few homes reached by long flights of steps stood high on the hillside above us.

Yet many homes and businesses below the sidewalk were on a strip of level land that rose gently, so gently it did not keep pace with the steepening road. In order to have an entrance on the sidewalk, buildings had to stand on higher and higher foundations. Looking between them I could see parts of the veneer company spread over the level land below, where, because the day was Sunday, no work was being done. Yet the mill was like a dog snorting in his sleep as he dreamed; Papa explained it was steam escaping from the boilers; Sunday or no, somebody must keep a head of steam; otherwise there'd be a long wait before the saws could start work on Monday morning.

Past the many buildings of the veneer company, I could see one side of Bunker Hill across the low land. Only a creek flowed along the far side, but the space between was wide and level as a river valley. Years later in a geology class I learned it was the old valley of the South Fork. Many millions of years ago, a bend of the South Fork almost reached the Cumberland on the far side of Bunker Hill, but she had twisted away to flow around in front of the hill and through the valley that now held much of lower Burnside.

A slow and intermittent rise of the land, known as the

Cincinnati-Nashville Dome, had affected much of the Cumberland River and many of her tributaries. As the land rose, the South Fork cut through the narrow neck of land separating her from the Cumberland on the far side of Bunker Hill, and left her old valley to enter the bigger river there.

However, as I walked to church, I didn't know what the word *geology* meant. We soon reached what I think of as the upper part of lower Burnside. The sidewalk had stopped climbing; across from us enough of the hillside had been dynamited out to make room for Dr. Gamblin's office and "hospital" and a few other buildings.

Just past these buildings, the road divided and the steep branch rose diagonally past raw bluffs blasted down to the rock. This road went up past the railway passenger station, and still climbing continued to the school building.

We stayed on the sidewalk by the low road. Here was what one might call the "business district," though nobody ever called it that. Several businesses were down near the rivers. Burton's restaurant and ice cream parlor, a small grocery store, and Dr. Stigall's office were in the upper town, but the larger retail stores, the dentist's office, livery stables, and other businesses were on or near the low street.

Past the split in the road, the old valley of the South Fork was almost level with the low road that now had a sidewalk and buildings on either side. But there was no time to look at anything: Mama, saying we would be late, hurried us across the street and up the stairway of Oakford Nunn's store.

I remember little of the church services held in the store. I enjoyed the hymns and was proud of papa because he sang bass in the choir. At first, the remainder of the service was only a dreary time of waiting for the end while sitting still as stone.

Several Sundays passed. I learned that after the benediction, my parents and the other grown-ups began shaking hands and talking to each other and to the preacher. This meant more waiting—until I grew bolder and the time of waiting became a time of expectancy.

I left the talking people to run down the stairs and begin my exploration of a part of Burnside. I had only to go a short distance past the store and without crossing the street to reach the pretty fence that surrounded the Seven Gables lawn. I walked on trying not to stare at the men sitting on what I supposed was the front porch. The sidewalk ended by a short uphill road that went only past Dick, Denney, and Van Hook Dry Goods. I did not cross the short road, but after looking in all directions, turned and walked past the Seven Gables again.

I went even more slowly than on my first trip past, for in addition to scrutinizing all of the side of the Seven Gables I could, from peaked roofs of high gables to the greening grass of the lawn, I stopped often to turn and look across the street at the Presbyterian Church and other buildings there. My slow walk eventually took me back past Oakford Nunn's store and to the split in the road.

Here I could see even more of the town, but on most Sundays I felt bold enough to cross the low road, and after trying to see through the several windows of darkened stores, I turned to walk past the Presbyterian Church. I lingered in front of the old church, wondering how men had been able to shape the blocks of stone that formed its walls, and wishing my parents were Presbyterians so that I could go inside. Sometimes I walked past the church, but never got out of sight of a certain door, the door across the street that led to the upstairs of Oakford Nunn's store. I looked at it often. Sooner or later, I would see church members coming out the door. This was the signal for me to run across the street as quickly as possible so that I could be waiting by the door when my parents came out.

4

HIGHER
IN LOWER BURNSIDE

Here and there i saw blooming roses, and all the trees in lower Burnside and on Bronston Hill were green—except the two in front of the post office. They appeared green only from a distance on a still day; when the wind blew, these two became pale ghosts of trees with no green about them. I took my wonders to Papa; he told me they were silver maples. Their leaves were silvery white on their undersides; this showed when the wind was right. Somebody had set them to beautify the post office. Mama thought it was the Burnside Garden Club.

Full spring that year was a wonderful time. The school term would soon be ending, but Elizabeth showed little joy because of this. During the last several weeks she had seldom cried when leaving for school. Some days she had seemed eager to go. At home her talk of school had become so filled with pleasant things that I became eager to go. She liked her teacher and was making excellent grades. She talked more of her classmates, mentioning many by name, and sometimes described for my benefit the games she took part in during recess.

Late spring brought still more happiness to Elizabeth and me. Mama had at last decided the weather was warm enough that we could quit wearing long underwear. I wore, as did most little girls, gingham or percale dresses up to my knees, and under the dresses bloomers made of the same material. During summer I had to wear only drawers under this outfit and go sockless in barefoot sandals. Summer Sundays found us in petticoats under dresses of organdy, dotted swiss, or some other thin white cotton material; with such dresses we wore patent leather slippers and white socks, and hats for church and Sunday school.

Elizabeth as a schoolgirl wore longer dresses and petticoats with bloomers or drawers that, unlike mine, were not supposed to show. Yet at the first hint of cold, often in October, we were crammed into heavy underwear that reached from neck to wrists and ankles. The short sleeves of summer gave way to long sleeves, while my sandals and slippers were replaced by ankle-high, round-toed shoes and heavy, black, ribbed stockings that reached to the bottoms of my bloomers. All this was a torture within doors and out on warmish days of spring and fall, especially when we had to wear our winter coats.

The pleasure of coming out of long underwear and feeling the spring winds on our bare legs was added to excitement when we learned the plans of our parents. First, Mama was giving up all plans she'd ever had for running a boardinghouse. Second, the family was moving again. We had lived in the house at the foot of the uphill road scarcely two months. That was too long for our mother. She had complained daily of being "shut-in" by the bluffs and steep hills and the morning fog. She blamed the foggy damp for the grippe that had kept her in bed for weeks; even our father had been bedridden for two or three days.

Papa was renting for our new home the upstairs rooms of a house belonging to Mrs. Alice Lewis, who owned the Seven Gables. Mama was vexed by having to live in only part of a house and share it with another family, and she still detested the location. The move took us only up the old valley of the South Fork near the end of the low street. Here we were farther from the river and the sounds of the lumber mills, but we still had Cumberland River fog, and instead of the river bluff we had the steep flank of Bunker Hill across the valley. Trains on the main line still roared and whistled above and behind us while the yard engine, nearing the beginning of its curve across the valley, was closer than before.

Our new home was well past the Seven Gables, which meant quite a trek to the post office, but not so far as to stop my usual errands. Now and then Elizabeth came with me, but with no woman to help, Mama usually needed Elizabeth to wash dishes, make beds, and do other work. I learned from going up and down the street more about the different buildings and the people who lived in them or worked in the stores and post office. Sight of the Seven Gables still dazzled me, but I was less taken with the large frame home on the opposite side of the road, even after I learned it was the Burnside House, heard of General Burnside, and understood the reason for the name of the house.

One of the most interesting places for me when walking by was the large, rambling home of the Fitzgeralds set some distance back from the sidewalk. Nearby was their woodworking shop. Here Oscar Fitzgerald and his father made many of the coffins used in the town and nearby country. It was said that under the black or white cloth of the coffins was sound hardwood of a good thickness with no thin, worm-eaten planks. The Fitzgeralds made other things also, and were known for beautiful cedar chests.

One afternoon when heat waves danced in the road and I could feel the heat of the sidewalk through my sandals, I was rewarded by the sight of the stagecoach, which came up just as I was leaving the post office. I stood and looked at the coach, the horses, the people, and the mailbags swinging from the back while the driver went into the post office, came out again to hang on more bags of mail, then got into his seat and drove away toward Monticello. This was the closest and longest look I had ever had, and though I didn't know it then, my last. Mr. Burton was already planning to buy another motor coach; the afternoon stage ran until 1915, but I somehow always missed seeing it.

I found our second home in the valley dull compared to the

45

first. There were fewer wagons and buggies traveling the road that continued southward to Tateville. Yet I could still hear all the sounds I had heard in lower Burnside and more, for we could hear the church bells and, on Sunday afternoons, the shouts and screams of baseball fans. The ball field was only a short distance up the road, the only uninhabited level piece of ground in the lower town big enough for a baseball field.

The clackety roar of trains and their whistles and bells were as loud as ever, but sounds of the mill whistles were somewhat muted. I was soon able to distinguish the loud whistle of Kentucky Lumber and the slightly weaker, shriller whistle of Chicago Veneer. Weaker toots came from Ayer & Lord Tie Company, the cedar mill, the spoke factory, Bauer Cooperage, and part of the time from an excelsior company.

Children enjoying aftersupper games in the streets knew it was time to stop their play and go home when the man at the waterworks blew the eight o'clock children's curfew. We played with the children of the Wright family next door, but spent more time at home playing with our dolls, ABC blocks, and other toys. Better than any play were the stories Elizabeth read to us or told when she had time. She didn't have much time left from the housework. Mama suffered much from attacks of what we and the neighbors called "sick headache," more commonly known as migraine. The attacks came often to last three or four days. During such times she remained in bed in a darkened room; we children tried to be church-quiet; the least noise, even the rustle of a newspaper, would cause her to scream with pain.

During the many days when quietness was demanded, Elizabeth would tell Peggy and me to play quietly on our front porch, the one for the second story. Our favorite pastime when on the porch was blowing bubbles. I had never cared for bubbles until I could blow and swing them over the porch railing and watch their flight. Sometimes one of mine or Peggy's would burst before reaching the ground, but now and then one would float all the way across the road. Other times we'd manage to hit the ice wagon or Mr. Colyer's meat wagon.

Early in the summer we saw a few people come by with

huckleberries for sale. Mama, if not too sick, would buy a gallon or so. These small wild fruit had a flavor not found in their bigger cultivated sisters, the blueberries now sold by grocers. The wild ones were greatly prized for jam and pies, but there were never enough to let each housewife buy all she wanted. Huckleberries did not grow in the immediate neighborhood of Burnside, but several miles away on the higher hills and ridges south and east of us. Those sold in Burnside had had to be carried the several miles on foot or muleback. The pickers usually lived far from a passable road.

Big juicy blackberries that ripened later bent down their tall briars along many streets and roads of the town and along the fencerows of nearby fields; they were a plague in pastures. People either picked their own or bought them out of the flood that came to town. Blackberries were used for jelly, jam, and pan or cobbler pies; a great many were canned by housewives in half-gallon glass jars. They were so much a part of life that they entered into several of the funny stories told by country people under the title of "The Preacher Who Dropped In for Dinner."

Sometime between the huckleberries and the blackberries, I began to waken to the sound of an argument carried on by our mother with repeated use of Papa's first name, Elias. I knew he was listening, though he seldom spoke. Several times I heard her say, "I can't go on living in this hot noisy place." Other times I heard her complain of the lack of a place for laying hens that would give us all the eggs we needed. Her biggest complaint, which Elizabeth and I often heard, was the lack of a barn in which to feed a cow and keep her at night.

I was glad we couldn't have a cow. It seemed to me there were already too many in Burnside. No matter where I went in the town, I had to be careful not to step in their sticky manure, nastier even than the horse or mule manure scattered in road crossings. Later, I heard stories of men out late with neither lantern nor flashlight who had stumbled into cows sleeping in the road.

Mama eventually told Elizabeth and me that Papa had bought about thirty acres of land from the Burnside Land

Company and was hiring carpenters to build a home for us. The land was in the Burnside school district; we could have a good school but live out of the noise and fog of the lower town, for the land was high up on one side of Tyree's Knob above the town, about a mile from school and two miles from our father's work. And where was Tyree's Knob? I had never heard of it. Mama said it was close on the backside and southeast of Burnside; we would learn all about it when we lived there.

The only mention in print I have ever found of Tyree's Knob is in a brochure published by the Seven Gables Hotel. It is undated, but we can reasonably assume it was published several decades ago; a room with a private bath and three meals daily cost only $17.50 per week. Most space is given to the delights afforded by the country around Burnside; the traveler while staying in the Seven Gables could fish in the Cumberland, visit nearby points of interest, or take walks on the many beautiful trails around Burnside. One of the walks mentioned led to Tyree's Knob, which afforded a "wide view of the surrounding country."

Two or three weeks later Papa took Elizabeth and me one Sunday afternoon to a spot in the upper town from which we could see one side of Tyree's Knob. But by that time I was no longer interested. I wanted to stay where we were. I had been sent on an errand to Mr. Matt Lloyd's General Store and had fallen in love with the place, which was a short distance up the valley road, and then across toward Bunker Hill.

Soon I was being sent on other errands to my favorite store. Smells from the barrels of coal oil that flanked the entrance greeted me as I neared the store. Much as I loathed the smell, I always stood for awhile to study the objects in the big, low "show windows"; behind the glass could be seen pitchforks, red glass bedside lamps, a patent churn, blue-banded white bowls, men's shoes, boys' caps, owl-decorated lamp chimneys, horse collars, mule shoes, and hames.

However, the objects that hypnotized me had nothing to do with any human need. These were two life-sized heads of decapitated Indian warriors whose fierce eyes, black hair, and reddish brown skin were made yet more ominous by the streaks of red on their cheeks and foreheads—until I looked at the bloody stumps of their necks. They probably bore little resemblance to any Indians who ever lived, but I could imagine those bloody heads being cut from their bodies, rolling away, blood dripping, like the heads of chickens Mama chopped off with an ax when she'd bought one for cooking. What had the Indians, I wondered, done to be treated so? Had they gone to heaven when they died?

I turned away with a mixture of goose pimples and sorrow. Going into the store, I found it quiet and shadowy, seemingly empty. It was then the smells were strongest: tobacco smoke and juice, new overalls, bananas, new leather, oranges, freshly cut ham, cheese, and fainter whiffs of other commodities. Soon I would see two or three men, sitting around the tall stove in the middle of the room. Errands took me to Mr. Lloyd's store many times during the next several years; summer and winter there were always two or three men sitting around the stove as on my early visits. Their low-voiced talk, interrupted by the opening of the door, would resume when they saw who had entered.

There was always time to look around. Even if not busy with other customers, Mr. Lloyd never rushed at me to ask what was wanted as if in a hurry to get me out of the store.

The first thing I saw, and what any customer would be apt to notice first, was the grocery counter to the right of the door. Mr. Lloyd didn't hide anything: within reaching distance of the counter was a barrel of crackers and other barrels of white sugar and brown, salt, beans, and vinegar, the last with a hand pump on top; in season there would be a barrel of apples and baskets of cabbages, turnips, and sometimes sun-dried apples.

There were stand-on scales on the floor and smaller ones on the counter. Nearby on the counter was a round of cheese that looked as big around as a wagon-wheel but a great deal thicker, and beside it a wide-bladed cleaver with which Mr. Lloyd could at one whack cut off the asked-for number of pounds or ounces. Under a curving glass counter top were the penny and two-for-a-penny candies: hoarhound and peppermint sticks, chocolate drops, sour balls, and other varieties of many colors and shapes, all unwrapped so the buyer could see what he or she was getting. On the floor near one end of the counter were baskets of Irish potatoes and, in season, sweet potatoes.

Canned goods occupied shelves behind the counter; in front of these, hanging by cords from a crossbar, were monstrous long and bulging bologna sausages, a few hams, a flitch or two of bacon, and most of the time a stalk of bananas.

Opposite the grocery counter were the many-drawered cabinets common to all the dry goods stores of the town. They held the usual assortments of thread, buttons, lace, and other small items. Past these were tables of clothing with bib-over-alls predominating. Shelves on the wall behind the tables held a variety of family needs from lamp wicks to wallpaper. Here also were window shades, coal oil lamps, fruit jars, boxes of extra tops and rings, and other boxes the contents of which I could only wonder on.

The back half of the store was a man's world, but when several customers were ahead of me, I could go there and pretend to be considering the few items a female could be interested in: patent churns, crocks, washtubs, and wash-boards could be found among the harness, singletrees, kegs of nails, steelyards, lanterns, hammers, axes, and other tools.

My business finished, I wanted to stay longer but I knew I dared not stay too long from home. I liked Mr. Lloyd. He treated me as if I were a grown person and never patted my head. I felt I was getting too old for pats.

The summer days around the end of blackberry time were long and hot, but the tedium was sometimes broken by the coming of the watermelon wagon. Big melons grown in a nearby river bottom, picked ripe from the vine the previous night and still pleasantly cool, could be had for five or ten cents. Our mother bought them to be cut and eaten in the backyard. Watermelons were not considered suitable for eating within the house as part of a meal and should be eaten immediately after cutting.

I think Elizabeth was very glad when September came and she could go back to Burnside Graded School. On the morning of the first day I heard the school bell, a sound I had never heard when we lived lower in the town.

Elizabeth had scarcely time to learn the best route to school from this second place in the valley before she had to learn a new and longer road to school from our new home on Tyree's Knob.

5

SETTLING
ON TYREE'S KNOB

We moved to our new home high on Tyree's Knob in mid-autumn of 1913. In spite of having two stories and an attic, the white-painted house looked small and out of place among the tall oaks, maples, and hickories that surrounded it. The house stood at the beginning of a narrow bench of level land that would become in the following spring the site of a vegetable garden, and later an orchard and small cornfield.

The level ground was bounded in back by a limestone cliff, irregular and broken so that in places it was easily climbed; above this, slopes of varying steepness led to the top of the hill. In front of the house the tree-covered land went down in slopes and ledges to Burnside after dipping low into a narrow creek valley and coming up again.

Our mother's eagerness to be out of lower Burnside had caused us to move before the house was finished. Except for a small kitchen stoop, it stood naked of porches, and these had to be built front and back, but they must wait for more important needs: an outhouse a good distance down the hill from the house; a cistern dug near the house; a paling fence for a garden and yard; and wire fence for a barn lot, orchard, and small fields. Now, with plenty of room, our mother planned on buying a milk cow or two. Thus a barn had to be built as well as a chicken house.

My main contribution to the work was the obeying of orders to keep out of the way. This meant going into the woods. I climbed the ledges behind the house and investigated the hill above where many different trees grew, with a few pines on the very top. Adjoining our place on the northern side was a tract of timberland owned by the Burnside Land Company. Though it had been cut over several years previously, there were still a good many oaks, hickories, and maples left because they were "wind-shook" or had some other defect that ruined them for lumber. The largest trees were the sycamores that grew only in a marshy place around the hill from our house.

Scattered through this woodland were tall slender hickory saplings. In time I learned to shinny up a tall one, swing around on the top, and at last, by taking the very tip, bend it to the ground. Sometimes in trying to climb up or down a rock ledge, I would scrape a knee or elbow, and get wounds I tried to keep hidden. Girls were not supposed to climb. There were a few low-limbed trees I could climb high to a swaying seat the better to see the sky and listen to the world around me.

The woods were never silent. During the rare times when I could feel no breeze, the pines that crowned the hill talked in low voices, and on windy days they roared and quarreled in loud tones. There was never enough noise in the woods to drown Mama's calling me to come take care of Peggy. Now and then on an especially still day I would hear a faint roaring that was neither a distant train nor the murmur of the pines. I would wonder as I listened and then forget it, until one cloudy Sunday morning I heard the same sound. I asked Papa what it was, and learned it was Cumberland River roaring her way down Smith Shoals.

Unless the wind was too loud in the trees, we could from the house hear all the mill whistles and church bells. On weekdays our mother would stop work to listen with mournful head-shakes when the tolling of a funeral bell came up to us. All the while she was counting the tolls; if only a few, there would be silence and sorrow for the unknown child; if a great many, she would say: "Well, whoever it was has lived the allotted three score years and ten."

The school bell was the most important bell of weekdays. The first bell that rang at eight o'clock meant it was time for my sister to make her last-minute preparations and start the mile-long walk to school. The second bell at eight-thirty meant the school doors were opening and children were lining up to go to their rooms.

A lonesome but pleasant sound was made by the trains blowing far away and without the clackety-clack. There was little silence between trains. During those years there were eight northbound and eight southbound passenger trains daily over what many Burnsiders called the Queen and Crescent. There were many more freights, both north and southbound.

In spite of having two engines, freights headed south had less steam for the required hoots than those northbound with only one engine. Cincinnati-bound freights were going downgrade and thus had steam to spare. On one of these the extra steam was used to whistle the drawn-out, wailing tones of "Jesus Loves Me."

However, I still had more of Burnside than her sounds. Sometimes on Saturdays I was sent with Elizabeth on errands, usually to a store or two, and always to the post office. Sundays, the two of us went with Papa to our temporary church in the valley. During these trips, I became better acquainted with a part of the upper town.

Our way led past the Baptist Church; opposite the church we turned the corner to follow a street where along with Dr. Stigall's home and office were several other homes. This street ended at the road that led down past the passenger station to the lower town. Coming or going we often had to stop to let a train pass. The train was not yet in sight when the warning bell clanged and jangled as Mr. McClain, the guard, let the barriers down. Seconds later we'd hear the whistle from down the line, and soon a double-header rounded the curve north of the depot to roar past us followed by a long line of boxcars. Northbound freights often hauled coal cars and flatcars stacked with lumber.

The shortest wait of all was for the through passenger trains that never stopped at Burnside. One of the most admired of these was on the Florida run; then known as Number Three when southbound and Number Four on the northbound run, it was soon named the Royal Palm. Made up of sixteen cars that included Pullmans, dining and club cars, and the usual coaches, baggage, and mailcars, the Royal Palm had, in addition to all the personnel carried for the comfort and convenience of her passengers, a hostess.

Those in and around Burnside who were going a long distance would take a local to Somerset where they could board the Royal Palm or one of the other through trains that included the Florida Sunbeam, the Suwannee River Special, and the Queen and Crescent.

The trains we watched pass at a given time were always much the same, but as the frosts hardened, the woods seemed to change from hour to hour. The maples growing in the rocks above the house were so bright they seemed to reflect the light of the afternoon sun. A harder frost stripped them and many other trees of their leaves. The mystery was soon gone from the woods; I could see quite a distance behind or ahead.

The oaks hung onto their leaves, but acorns of many varieties fell like rain. I hunted one of each size; their shine and smoothness below their curious cups were pleasant to see and feel. I hunted hickory nuts to eat during the winter and learned the hard way to gather only the big, thin-shelled nuts from a variety of scale bark hickory.

The most fun was playing "dead man" in the leaves with Elizabeth when she was home from school and on the rare times when Mama, who was feeling very poorly, didn't need her help. "Dead man" could not be played alone. We took turns being the corpse to be buried in a mound of leaves. The grave digger was also the preacher who gave the funeral sermon while the corpse lay silent under the leaves. If the sermon seemed overlong to the corpse, or if she felt she might be sharing her grave with a big woolly worm or a snake, she had the right to spring out of the grave to become a ghost. The preacher, feigning terror, would scream for all she was worth and run, while the ghost chased her in and out among the trees. It was great fun except when Peggy was around and we scared her half to death.

Sometimes when we played through the twilight and into the early darkness, we would stop our game and each try to be the first to see a star, meanwhile repeating the old and well-known rhyme:

> Star light, star bright,
>> First star I see tonight,
> I wish I may, I wish I might
>> Have the wish I wish tonight.

It was a dangerous game; there was always the chance of seeing a falling star. That meant somebody was dying.

Our father, at our mother's insistence, had felled the trees on either side of the house and for a considerable distance down the hill in the little spare time he had from his work at Chicago Veneer.

Our mother had her wish for a good view, and as the leaves fell, the view widened. Lower Burnside was hidden under the brow of the hill, but we could see parts of upper Burnside, the graveyard, a stretch of the Cumberland below Burnside, the fields on top of Bunker Hill, and farther away, more fields and farmhouses on the high Bronston plain. Beyond Bronston, the land stretched away to lines of low hills, blue against the sky.

We could on many mornings trace the bends of the Cumberland for several miles by the fog that rose above it. Other mornings all the world below us lay under a sea of white fog with wisps around the hill, and when Elizabeth left for school she was quickly swallowed in the white sea. Only the top of the hill behind and above us would be clear. The view from our home and the front yard, wide as it was, let us see only from northwest to southwest with the longest views straight west. We had glorious sunsets, but never a sunrise, of which Mama often complained.

One afternoon Elizabeth brought a letter from Granma Denney. Mama read and with a pleased look told us Granma would visit us soon. I was as eager as Mama for her coming.

She somehow added excitement and change to our lives; Mama always seemed to feel better when her mother was with us. At the same time I was afraid of Granma Denney; she was much stricter in matters of manners and dress than Mama.

A few days later I was playing on the hill above the house when I looked out and down to the school path. There was a woman dressed all in black silk that glistened in the sun. It was Granma Denney, dressed as usual when traveling or going to church. She was carrying her coat, while walking behind her was a good-sized boy with her grip. She looked up, saw me and our house, took the grip, and put something into the boy's hand. Moments later I had reached her. She held out her arms, and I was enveloped in the long, full-skirted dress and black-clad arms.

We stood back to look at each other. I was happy to see nothing about her was changed; and she still wore the mammoth, long-tailed black silk bonnet that made her eyes seem black instead of gray.

I took her coat, and as we walked up the path, she asked how Papa was getting along. The question surprised me; I took Papa's health and strength for granted and never thought of his being tired as Mama often was. I told Granma he was fine. She shook her head over Papa, I thought, and then asked how Mama was feeling. I told her Mama hadn't had a spell of sick headache in a long time, but was often sick at her stomach mornings and was feeling poorly. Granma was nodding as if I had given an expected answer.

When Mama, with Peggy at her heels, reached us, Granma's talk was all with her as they walked to the house, where Mama shook down the ashes in the cookstove, built up the fire, and put on a pot of fresh coffee. Granma stopped her from cooking anything. No, she wasn't hungry. No, she wasn't tired enough to lie down. She'd come from Monticello in the motor coach; at the Burnside depot a man who seemed to know her had given her a ride to the Antioch Road, and the boy with him had carried her grip.

She left the room. I waited until she returned and was happy to see her housework outfit was the same as I remembered. Her clothing varied a bit from day to day, but was always black and white: a black percale dress sprigged with white, or white sprigged with black, and over these, large aprons usually white with black figures. The patterns were always small, meet for a woman who'd been a widow for over thirty years.

I continued to hang around while she and Mama talked between sips of coffee. Coffee finished, she took from her apron pocket what I had been waiting to see—black knitted mitts. Most people, including Mama and Granma Denney, wore gloves to church, and in cold weather all of us wore mittens or gloves, but Granma's mitts, covering only the backs of her hands and palms with more than half of each finger left bare, were the only ones I had ever seen. She wore them constantly except when eating or cooking. She had not changed.

I had put on my best behavior and continued to wear it as carefully and consciously as a new Sunday dress. There were a few slipups. One day Mama directed me to sweep the little side porch. The broom was not in its accustomed place. I asked, "Where's the broom at?" Granma answered, "You'll find it behind the 'at.'" Elizabeth and I both were reprimanded for not standing straight and more often for slouching as we sat. The slouches came mostly during the evenings while Elizabeth read a story to me after we had finished washing the supper dishes. We'd sit by a little kitchen table with a lamp in the middle while she read as I listened, often to a story I had already heard but wanted to hear again. I especially liked "The King of the Golden River" and "The Nuremberg Stove."

Elizabeth would be leaning above the book on the table and I leaning as close as possible when Granma Denney would come. She never said anything until the story was finished, and then we'd get a little lecture on sitting straight, followed by the suggestion that we sit or walk with books on our heads. We did so and discovered the least slouching would send the books to the floor.

She would sigh for the days when girls were kept straight with backboards. Elizabeth would just sigh. I never thought about it then, but she must have been tired. The walk from the school to the post office was a mile; home from the post office was two more miles, uphill most of the way. At home Mama kept her so busy she had little chance to sit down until supper.

It was only in the woods that I didn't have to watch my posture and my tongue, but in late November the expected rain came and the woods were lost to me. The gray sky seemed to sit on top of our house, and out of it the slow, cold rain fell steadily night and day as if it meant never to stop. The constant drizzle got on our mother's nerves, but pleased our father. He said we needed a long hard rain to bring a good tide to the Cumberland so that steamboats could again get in and out of Burnside; more rain would raise the creeks and rivers above Burnside, and logs could then get down to the mills. All were getting low on timber.

The weather obliged Papa by sending another long steady rain. Soon we were hearing the lonesome-sounding, long-drawn notes of steamboat whistles, but by then there was the excitement of the first snow; big-flaked and wet, it didn't last long. Sorrow for its disappearance was lost in the fun of getting ready for Christmas. Granma and I made many decorations for the tree we children chose—a fat cedar that Papa cut from our woods one Sunday afternoon. I thought it beautiful with the decorations and real candles.

Christmas brought the usual toys, including a fancy-dressed and long-haired doll that would open and close her eyes. After Christmas came New Year's Day of 1914. New calendars were all over the house. I understood 1913 was gone. I was sorry. I had heard talk of three great events in Burnside in 1913 and had not seen one of them.

First was the unusually high tide that had soaked lower Burnside before we moved from Bronston. The second was the wreck of a freight that had scattered boxcars all over the hillside. Nobody had been hurt, so it would have been a fine spectacle, or so I thought. Wrecks like floods were common in Burnside, and so were fires. The third great event was a fire that had destroyed what was still called the old academy, though no school had been taught there for years.

I heard talk of these misfortunes and others during the days when bad weather kept me in the house with Granma Denney, Mama, and Peggy. I didn't always have time to listen. When Granma learned that I did not yet know all my numbers and could not count to one hundred she was scandalized. Finished helping with the housework and cookery, she would settle herself with the lace she was knitting while I worked, under her direction, on learning my numbers.

I was glad when she stopped knitting lace and turned to quilt piecing. Knit of number eighty white sewing thread, her lace was the biggest fault—and about the only one—I found in Granma Denney. The lace was a series of points about two inches long when finished; it was used as edging on the tops and bottoms of our Sunday petticoats and the bottoms of our drawers. Starched and ironed into stiffness, the petticoat tops cut into my flesh on summer Sundays and made old chigger bites itch until I could scarcely sit still.

I wanted to help in the quilt piecing, but Granma thought I ought to piece a quilt of my own. It was time I learned to sew; I could make a nine-patch on the sewing machine. Granma cut each of the nine small squares that went into a block. Too short to sit and sew, I stood on one foot and worked the sewing machine treadle with the other. It was great fun deciding what color should go with another and sewing away. At such times I had the added enjoyment of listening to the women talk as they sewed by hand, though our mother did most of the talking; she could talk while doing any work except fancy embroidery or crochet.

Shortly after the New Year, seed catalogs came in the mail. Mama spent much time in studying them and discussing varieties of flowers and vegetables with Granma. The seed were decided upon at last and ordered. Talk of other matters was resumed.

Mama never wearied of her memories "back in Wayne County" where she'd been born and lived until a few years after her marriage. She had grown up surrounded by her dead father's relatives—the Denneys. Granma Denney's people, the Fosters and other families, had all gone to farm Missouri land shortly after Granma's marriage. Mama talked of this

Denney or that one, her old beaux, life as a schoolgirl, and later as a teacher: pupils she had had, homes she had boarded in, teachers' examinations, and the pleasures of the Teachers' Institutes held in Monticello for several days each year. Memories she loved as much as or more than those of the Institutes were of the horses she had ridden and owned. She talked of them by name and discussed the characteristics of each as if they had been members of the Denney clan.

Sometimes I wearied of her talk and turned the pages of books to look at the pictures, but could find interest in nothing except the thought of playing in the snow or walking through the woods in the rain. Such pleasures were denied me most of the time because during the winter months I was labeled "a puny child." I had colds followed by earaches and sometimes what was called tonsillitis—known today as a throat infection. This ailment brought fever and usually Dr. Stigall.

I was always glad when after much cogitation and consideration of the weather Mama and Granma agreed I might go for the milk and butter we bought from an old couple who lived with a young, unmarried relative known as Miss Laura. It was a pleasant walk along an old road around the hill to the old Tyree home where the people lived.

The old man never said much of anything except "Howdy, little neighbor," but the old woman was always eager for conversation—or simply the chance for talk, especially of witches and witchcraft. There were days when she'd tell me in whispers of the hard time some women had with their churnings; they thought the churning was so bewitched that the butter wouldn't come. One woman was certain it was the same evil one who had bewitched her cow so bad that for days she wouldn't give down her milk, and who had nigh killed one of her horses by choking him with a witch's ball.

I never did learn what a witch's ball was, but I did learn how to get rid of a witch who was doing me evil—or of any other wicked person. The method she whispered to me was the same known to ancient peoples and to millions today: make a doll—wax works best if you've got it—and do to that doll what you think ought to be done to the evil person; kill it if need be.

The trouble with this method for me was that I couldn't make a doll in the likeness of a witch or an evil person when I didn't know any. I had sense enough not to ask at home for the name of a witch. I listened, hoping Granma and Mama would talk of witches, but they never did.

Sometimes when Granma Denney and Mama were talking of the old days when Granma's mother was a girl they'd get going on fearsome tales of the wild hogs, wolf packs, and wildcats that frightened and sometimes killed children hunting sheep in lonesome places or walking paths to neighbors' houses. Worse than these were the stories of fearful encounters with copperheads and rattlesnakes, and of boys who disobeyed their parents to swim or wade in millponds and died of water moccasin bites.

Other times I'd hear talk of the wars and the hardships our people had lived through for many generations. Granma Denney had hair-raising tales of Indian attacks on long-gone ancestors who had lived "on the other side of the mountains a long time ago before the Revolution."

There were stories of the Revolution and the War of 1812, not of battles, but of returning soldiers and of those who did not return, and of women working and waiting at home. The saddest and most terrible stories were the handed-down tales of The War, with many fearful accounts of guerrilla wickedness.

I disliked the talk of old wars and was glad they stopped when it was time to start supper. Peggy and I were not supposed to follow Mama; she didn't want us underfoot while she was cooking. I spent much of the late afternoon staring through the western windows, watching for Elizabeth to come up the school path. Sometimes I would run down to meet her and learn the news of school and Burnside. Later, often while balancing books on my head, I would stand by a front window watching for the glimmer of Papa's lantern down the hill, and then his shape coming out of the dark.

Quite often after the lamps were lighted, Granma Denney would make shadow pictures on the wall for us. She could bend and fold her fingers and thumbs in many ways; sometimes the shadow would be a duck's head opening and closing its bill; other times two ducks pecking at each other; a refolding of her fingers would give us a mule's head with long wiggling ears, or some other animal. Peggy squealed with laughter while Elizabeth and I enjoyed the show and begged for more.

The dark had deepened before our father came home from work, bringing the *Cincinnati Post* and news of Burnside and the rivers. Several weeks passed while news of the river remained much the same except for the names of steamboats that had come and gone.

Supper eaten, dishes washed, and kitchen straightened by my sister and me while our elders sat around the heating stove in another room to read or talk of happenings in the wider world, it was time to hope for a story from Papa. He was the best storyteller of all, and usually told us at least one after he had finished the paper and something he wanted to read in the *Saturday Evening Post*. He didn't read this magazine as much as our mother, but always wanted the stories by Irvin S. Cobb.

Reading finished, if it were not too late in the evening, he would tell us a story. Many were of the Revolution and handed down from ancestors who had fought in that war or stayed out of it because they were Tories but had no wish to fight neighbors or relatives. These stories, like those of the "Lost State of Franklin" and Swift's silver mine, were sometimes funny, often sad, but never grisly.

He was also a rare teller of ghost tales in which fiddles made music with no players anyone could see; spirits of the dead visited the living; ghost horses galloped and neighed as they passed travelers out late at night, and empty houses filled with ghostly sounds. In the telling, he gave us moans and the sounds of footsteps, creaking doors, and clanking chains. We would go shivering to bed unless he added some lighthearted tales such as that of "The-man-who-thought-he-could-do-his-wife's-work-better-than-she-did-it." Our favorite story with a happy ending was his version of "Jack and the Beanstalk," in

63

which he roared like the giant with a "Fee Fi Fo Fum, I smell the blood of an Englishman," and imitated all other characters.

The wintry weather was always changing. Rain or snow would be followed by hard cold that froze the mud and scattered the clouds. I could then watch the sun going down and later the evening star hanging above Bronston. Other times snow fell in big wet flakes that stacked up to whiten the world, only to disappear within a few days of warm sun or rain.

Our father's nightly reports were chiefly of rising rivers; the log booms were getting in good shape; there'd be plenty of timber to keep Burnside's mills going. I asked what a log boom was. He tried to explain. I had seen a log boom from the hill in the lower town, but hadn't known what it was. I still wanted to see one close up.

One evening after more rain, Papa told us the Cumberland was out of her banks, coming down wild and still rising. No, he explained to our worried mother, the tide wouldn't be high enough to do much damage; compared to last year's flood it was nothing. Somewhere upriver there had been a heavy downpour, but it hadn't been over a territory big enough to cause a good-sized flood in Burnside. Mostly, fast and sudden as it was, the rise was making a lot of hard work for boom hands and log drivers.

I so pestered him with questions on log booms and boom hands that he promised to take Elizabeth and me some Sunday after church to see the Cumberland River boom, but not until things had quieted down in lower Burnside.

6

GREAT EVENTS

TIME TO GO SEE the log boom seemed slow in coming. It was a sunny Sunday in early March before I at last had my wish. The Cumberland was still so high that we stood on the top of the bank at the head of the boom a short distance above the Somerset Road ferry. I hadn't thought there were so many logs in the world. Row upon row of logs stretched above the boom chains until they were lost in a curve of the river above the railway bridge.

The logs were like a floor the swift, muddy Cumberland didn't want. They were restless, groaning as they rubbed against one another, or one seemed to be trying to get on top of another. Some floated high and some floated low. Still they stayed in their places, and all were bigger logs than any that could have been made from any tree I had ever seen. I was further stunned when Papa explained that most of the logs in this boom belonged to Kentucky Lumber. The veneer mill's boom was over in the South Fork. The logs in that boom were bigger than these and floated higher because many were poplar.

Looking at the logs, I thought of the trees around home. They were alive; these logs were dead; dead as the Indians in Mr. Lloyd's store. I didn't want to look at so many corpses anymore, and ran to watch the roily, foam-flecked river at the ferry. Papa was explaining something to Elizabeth, but soon missed me and came to say we must be going; we'd make Sunday dinner too late for our mother.

It was many years later, when the great log booms around Burnside had become a part of the past, before I learned enough to understand what I had seen at the river. The learning came from Ross Kreamer who after working for several years in the veneer mill became president of the company in 1927 and remained until Lake Cumberland was ready to swallow lower Burnside; by that time veneer was in his blood, and he set up a hardwood veneer business in Memphis, Tennessee. From there he wrote: "Now, a boom is a fence in one sense of the word in the river. They drive a spike with a hole in the top into the end of each log and then thread a steel cable through each spike. They used big logs of low grade that would float. A lot of logs could be stored in a boom. Then the logs could be pulled up the river bank by a log chain to the log yard."

However, after being shoved into a creek or river, the logs didn't just quietly float down to Burnside and take their places in a boom. "Men walked the banks," Mr. Kreamer wrote, "with pike poles pushing them or with peavies turning the logs to keep them moving. This was one of the hardest of all jobs. It was cold and they were wet most of the time and by dark they were ready to fall down. Some evenings they'd find a log cabin nearby; here they'd spend the night and pay the man for room and food; on most such nights these men, four to six in a crew, would sleep on the floor in front of the fireplace. More often, with no house to be seen, they built a big fire and just slept on the ground without supper. They could not carry much with them."

In many stretches of the river, sheer bluffs rise straight above the water, so close as to force a man to walk in the water. Walking along the scattered strips of bottomland was little better; here mud and wet sand sucked down the boots of the men. Other times they had to walk over logs in the river. Mr. Kreamer wrote: "The logs would jam up and get crosswise and had to be unravelled and kept moving. When the logs reached Burnside there was another crew to guide them into the boom." These men also used pikes and peavies, and the soles of their boots were filled with sharp spikes to give a firmer footing when they had to walk logs in the river in order to shape the boom.

Ms. Bernice Mitchell, who came to Burnside as a child and later worked for Ayer & Lord Tie Company, remembers the rafts of ties that used to come down the rivers to Burnside. A raft, sometimes made up of twelve hundred ties, had to be well pinned together with poplar or hickory saplings in order to hold together in the swift and rough water of Buck Creek or a comparable tributary. The ties were hewn, usually by the owners of the timber, from white or red oak, and since none of the oaks will float to any extent, seasoned pine or some other light-weight wood had to be mixed with the ties.

Many ties came down to the two tie companies in Burnside, for many were needed; Ayer & Lord alone shipped ties to the New York Central, the Pennsylvania, and of course the Southern railways.

Cold, wet, and hungry raftsmen were no doubt relieved when their rafts of ties were safely delivered to a Burnside company. Yet timber in the river wasn't always secure. Now and then when the rivers were high and swift, rafts could break up; logs coming downriver, riding high and swiftly, would sweep over the booms and be gone downriver. At such times all men who could do anything at all with a log loose in the river were called out to help the boom hands.

Mrs. Clifton Thompson, Jr., of Lexington has vivid memories of such a time as seen through a young girl's eyes. The family had moved to Burnside around 1922 after Henry Gable (her father) and S. J. Glanton bought Chicago Veneer. Mr. Gable was down by the river seeing to this and that, while in the Gable home high above the lower town Mrs. Gable and Mrs. Glanton worked all night making coffee and doughnuts, at intervals taking loads down to the wet, shivering, worn-out men in and by the river. The boom hands and others worked all that night and the next day and the next night.

Runaway logs would usually come to rest somewhere down the Cumberland and could be towed back by launches. The big worry was for the boom hands. There were no floodlights to guide the men who with uneasy footing on floating logs worked with their long-handled pikes or peavies to get other logs to shore or into the boom. Yet they managed without any great mishaps.

Other men and boys helped in different ways. Lindley Mitchell remembers: "The Newell brothers and others used skiffs to row out and pull the logs to shore by one sitting in the rear of the boat with a pickaxe; the log was towed to shore by the pickaxe driven into one end; on shore a wedge with a ring in it was driven into each log and they were strung together like a catch of fish."

Worse than logs riding over the boom was a broken boom. This seldom happened, but Mr. Kreamer remembers such a time. "A log boom broke loose during a flood and down the Cumberland it went—when it got to Nashville it had collected a lot of logs and trash, and took out all the docks at Nashville." He further relates that the city of Nashville brought suit against a company in Burnside, but when the timber turned out to belong to another company, the suit was dropped.

Not all timber came *down* the rivers. The veneer company, for example, used its launches to tow bargeloads of timber up the Cumberland, and with the barges it used another craft equipped with a derrick for loading the logs. Ross Kreamer remembers many trips down the Cumberland to pick up logs left in piles by the river. There was beside each pile a fruit jar with a note inside from the owner telling the number of logs in the pile. Logs loaded onto the barges, payment in cash was put inside the jar and left where the logs had been. Nobody ever heard of anyone bothering the money until the owner, days or weeks later, returned to claim it.

A week or so after seeing the Cumberland River log boom, I awakened one morning to daylight spilling into the room. I was certain I had slept through Mama's get-up call; now I wouldn't see Papa; he left for work in the dark. I ran downstairs, hoping. I passed through the room with the heating stove. Mama was there, not doing anything, just walking back and forth. I went into the kitchen. Elizabeth was stirring the oatmeal and watching a skillet of frying ham. I asked if Papa had gone to work. She shook her head and told me he was shaving on the back porch.

Mystified, I wanted to ask questions, but just then Granma Denney came into the kitchen. She lectured me a bit on running around "not decently dressed," while fixing a pan of hot soapy water. At least it felt hot as she scrubbed my face with special attention to my neck and ears. Finished, she told me to go upstairs and put on clean clothing "from your skin out."

I obeyed as quickly as possible, eager to find out what was going on. Maybe we were moving again. Things were still strange when I went downstairs. We ate breakfast without Mama. The biscuits were higher and lighter than common; I knew Granma Denney had made them.

Breakfast finished, Granma told Elizabeth she'd do the dishes while Elizabeth fixed her school lunch. Granma combed Elizabeth's hair with never a pull, though Mama wasn't doing a thing but walking around in another room. They both hurried Elizabeth off to school in spite of her complaints of leaving too early; the first bell hadn't rung.

Elizabeth gone, Granma inspected me, combed my hair, and, as she put my winter coat to warm, told me I could go for the milk and butter now and visit with Miss Laura and the old people all day. Mama chimed in from another room with the command I take Peg with me.

I didn't want to go. What would I do all day? I knew it was hopeless to argue. Granma was already working Peg over. Papa helped by carrying Peggy and holding my hand as we walked up and around the lane, but he couldn't stop my wonder and disgust at being sent out in the raw cold with a gray sky overhead and grayer mud and rocks under my feet.

The old couple and Miss Laura added to my mystification by acting as if they were expecting us. I was sorry when Miss Laura left for Burnside shortly after we came. The day was long but could have been worse. The old man and Peggy took to one another at once. Mostly, she stayed with him in the room with a fireplace. I spent my time in the kitchen with the old woman and helped her make a high stack cake of many thin layers, each cooked in an iron skillet on top of the stove, then put together and covered with a brown-sugar icing.

It was getting on to suppertime and I was helping gather eggs and planning to help in the milking when Miss Laura came back with the report I had a new baby sister. Our "washerwoman" had found her in the woods and had brought her to Mama. Miss Laura seemed to think I ought to be happy at such a whopping tale. First, we didn't have a real "washerwoman"; there was a woman who came sometimes to help when Mama was feeling too poorly to do her work, but she wouldn't be out in this weather. Furthermore, I didn't need a baby sister.

Miss Laura carried Peg most of the way home. Nearing the house, I saw buggy tracks in the lane; the "washerwoman" had no buggy. Elizabeth was alone in the kitchen. She looked as if she had been crying. She told me we had a new sister and that Mama was sick in bed, asleep now, so we'd better be quiet.

Mama was in bed for three or four weeks; she thought she might be taking pneumonia. Dr. Stigall—we, like his other patients, called him Dr. Nick—had to come and see her. Papa looked worried. The new baby, named Lucy, slept. Peggy cried. She was beginning to learn she wasn't the baby anymore.

As Mama improved, so did the weather. Wind and sun together dried patches of earth higher up the hill. I found these, and Granma and I went together to fill the shallow wooden boxes in which Mama planned to plant cabbage, tomato, and pepper seed. We planted each after the boxes of earth had warmed awhile in the house.

The plot of ground that was to be the garden changed slowly from black mud to dry earth. Mama was up and around before a man with plows and team could come to plow the garden. The seed Granma and I had planted in the boxes had changed into plants almost big enough to set.

Mama was able to supervise the gardening and to plant some of the seed herself. Granma said Mama would kill herself by working in the cold earth. Mama said the smell of the freshly plowed ground made her feel better. Still she quarreled about the lateness of the season—too late for peas, Irish potatoes, lettuce, and radishes. She planted them anyway, and soon more vegetables.

The days were longer now; Papa used the daylight left when he got home from work to set out apple and peach trees. It never occurred to me that he could be tired after the long day's work and the two-mile walk up the hill, for he sang and whistled as he went about setting the fruit trees.

The wished-for cow came at last, a mean-looking Jersey with horns, and a feisty little calf that wouldn't let us pet him. I regretted the coming of the cow; she meant no more trips to see my friends around the hill.

Granma Denney sowed the seeds of marigolds, moss roses, old maids, and pretty-by-nights in small boxes of earth kept mostly indoors. Later, they would be set in beds near the house. Everybody helped in setting roses, iris, tansy, and other flowers and herbs. We also soon had chickens; some were cross old hens that would do nothing but sit on "settings" of eggs until they hatched.

Spring had come, but it was not yet time to get out of long underwear, take down the heating stove, and turn the house inside out for cleaning. The redbud and dogwood bloomed all over the hillsides, and once again I wandered in the woods— when I could escape our mother. I had been given to understand I was now old enough to help. One of my chores was keeping the woodbox in the kitchen filled with seasoned hickory or oak to be carried from the pile a short distance from the house. It seemed to me the stove used a prodigious amount of wood. You couldn't blame the stove; known as a six-cap range, it also had a hot water reservoir, a warming oven so high on the enameled back I could scarcely reach it, and a giant oven with ribbons and flowers outlined on the heavy iron door.

When I did manage to get away alone, I usually ran to the little swale where the beeches grew on either side of a spring. Here, between the beeches were great beds of flowers of many shapes and colors: yellow, white, and shades of blue and pink. I carried samples home to Granma to learn their names; yellow adder's-tongue, and creeping iris were among the first to bloom, but they had not closed their petals before hepaticas, anemones, wild blue phlox we knew as "Sweet William," red-brown trillium, jack-in-the-pulpit, mayapple, and several others were in bloom.

My life was interrupted by a suggestion from Granma that I felt amounted to a command; tomorrow if we had good weather she planned to visit Counsins Emma, Mollie, and Dora, and see Cousin Joe's wife. Our cousins, older than Mama but not as old as Granma, had climbed the hill one fine spring day to see the new baby, enjoy the view, and visit with Mama and Granma. They were three sisters, cousins of my long-dead Grandfather Denney, no relation to Granma Denney and far removed from me; yet all of us cousined each other.

Scrubbed, starched, and ironed, loaded with warnings from Mama to "behave," I went with Granma the next afternoon to the big frame house on a great sloping lawn, one in a row of large homes above the railway with Mrs. Phillippi's home on the closer end and Norman I. Taylor's at the further end. I liked the house with its many porches, curlicues on the eaves, and high-ceilinged rooms with high, narrow double windows that admitted little light because most of the time the curtains were drawn and the green shutters closed.

Cousin Mollie Dick, a widow, lived with her sister, Emma, who had married Mr. Van Hook when he was a widower with a grown daughter, Ollie Crow Van Hook. Cousin Dora and her husband, "Preacher" Taylor, lived in a smaller house behind the big one, and Cousin Joe, brother to the ladies and lately married to Grace Lewis, lived next door.

There were no children; the three Denney women had never had any. I received much attention and was careful to wear my churchly behavior. The home gave me an even greater feeling of church than being downtown in Dick, Denney and Van Hook Dry Goods, owned by Cousin Mollie, her brother Joe Denney, and Mr. Van Hook.

The room in which we sat seemed filled with twilight and

glimmerings from the dark polished furniture and the glass panes in the doors of the tall bookcases. I wondered if the big books had pictures but never asked. I spoke only when spoken to, usually to answer a question, and was careful to use "ma'am" when I felt it was needed; when Preacher Taylor and Cousin Dora came over to see us I got in some "sirs."

They forgot me and talked among themselves of old days in Wayne County, of friends and relatives, and of the store begun by their father "back before The War" at Mill Springs when his stock of goods had come from Nashville by steamboat.

I was glad when Cousin Mollie asked if I wouldn't like to go sit in a swing on the front porch. Here I could see the top of Bunker Hill and a stretch of Cumberland River.

Shortly after this visit when her moss roses were beginning to bloom, Granma Denney returned to Wayne County. Elizabeth and I helped her to the railway station where we waited for Mr. Burton's motorcoach. We cried all the way home.

Home wasn't the same without Granma Denney, but with the gardening, another baby to tend, and the cow that meant churnings, there was little time to sit and mourn. We didn't often get to enjoy the swing Papa had made on a big limb of a nearby oak. The grapevine swing on the edge of the bluff above the house was more fun, but I was seldom allowed to go there. We had only to cut the vine, grab the hanging part with both hands, and swing out and over the rocks several feet below, knowing as we swung that if we lost our grip we'd fall and break our bones. A year or two later, Peggy fell from such a swing and broke her arm.

One job I did because I enjoyed it was going around to see how each small tree Papa had planted was making out. It was a pleasure to see the fruit trees grow, while among the peach trees below the house I could peer down into the dark mouths of seemingly bottomless sinkholes, or better, look for little shells and other signs of life in the dead rocks. I asked Mama about these. She said they were called fossils; she didn't know their names. Longer ago than either of us could imagine, all this land had been at the bottom of a sea where the shells I found had covered live animals. I wondered and couldn't understand, but continued to hunt the strange little shells.

A few years later, I saw around the hill from our house two strange young men pecking at a limestone ledge with curious little hammers. I hurried home to ask what they were doing on the land company's land. Mama wasn't certain. When Papa came home from work he said he thought they were geology students. The University of Michigan had a summer school camp for geologists and their students down at Mill Springs. The men there spent a lot of time examining the rocks and earth for miles around.

Geologist? I wondered if a girl could be one.

Full summer came with heat waves dancing on the rocks and the kitchen scorching hot with canning. Blackberries finished, Mama would begin on green beans from the garden with now and then a batch of beet or cucumber pickles. Soon there'd be more tomatoes than we could eat; that meant more canning. Granma's flowers were all in bloom. Now and then a roaring thunderstorm with lightning crackling close would bring a bit of coolness as well as excitement. At such times, with Mama giving a quick example, we were ordered to sit on the floor with feather cushions or pillows under us.

One week, after I no longer heard steamboat whistles, I heard the sound of music that tore at my heart. It came from the level land near Mr. Lloyd's store. I ran to ask what it could be. Mama said that the "trashy carnival" was back again. Elizabeth and I begged to go, but Mama wouldn't even consider it and told us to be quiet. We missed all the yearly carnivals as well as the films shown in the Picture Palace in the lower town.

The long summer twilights were almost always cool and pleasant; the pretty-by-nights opened their white flowers, and as darkness thickened we watched the lightning bugs and listened to the whippoorwills calling from nearby trees. Soon, as full summer came on, we could scarcely hear the whippoorwills for the hundreds of katydids that called in loud shrill voices, "katydid," "katydidn't," from the trees around the

74

house. We learned from Papa we could silence a tree full by hitting the trunk with a rock or piece of wood. Elizabeth and I could silence them, tree by tree, but there were many trees around, and by the time we had shut up the last tree, the katydids had started up again in the trees first struck. During most of the summer we fell asleep to the sound of katydids.

My sixth birthday came and went during blackberry-canning time. Mama baked a cake. Elizabeth chanted for my benefit:

> School days, school days
>> Dear old black and blue days.
>> Reading, writing, and arithmetic
>> Taught to the tune of a hickory stick.

I didn't mind her chant; I was eager to find out what school was like.

Mama kept Elizabeth busy in the kitchen during canning time. That meant I had to do one of her biggest jobs, taking care of Lucy when she cried and Mama was busy and knew the baby wasn't hungry. Elizabeth could carry her around over her shoulder. I was not even permitted to pick her up for fear I would let her fall. Lucy, now about six months old, was a handful, wriggling and kicking. I could rock her only after Mama put me in the rocking chair; then, afraid I'd fall out because my feet didn't touch the floor, she tied me in.

This didn't keep me from rocking. I could rock and soon learned that by bending my body and swinging my legs, I could make the chair go forward or backward as it rocked. Thus, Lucy and I could travel from one wall to another or, much to Mama's consternation, into the kitchen. Peggy, too, had learned to rock herself in a small rocking chair.

Canning was finished, or so I thought—Mama would make sauerkraut and green tomato catsup just before frost. Still later, she'd can some of the sausage made from the two hogs fattening in a pen at the back of the garden, and she had not yet finished making jams, jellies, and preserves. The temporary halt in canning meant less wood to carry in for the stove, but I continued to spend what seemed eternities lifting the churn dasher up and down or rocking Lucy. Mama was making school clothing for Elizabeth and me. Two of the magazines to which she subscribed sold patterns for women's and children's clothing. Now and then Mama ordered a pattern, but most of the time she worked from the picture and description in the magazine. My school clothing was much like Elizabeth's; no more rompers—instead petticoats to be worn over underdrawers or bloomers and long underwear in cold weather. All girls big and little wore hair ribbons of some description, which meant more lengths of wide ribbon for me. Enough of my front hair was cut to make a fringe of bangs. The remainder was left uncut, but behind the bangs my top hair was gathered together and tied to form a small ponytail dangling down the back of my head. A bow made of wide stiff ribbon was fastened to the tie so as to stand high on the crown of my head.

Aside from Mama's sewing and an occasional reminder from Elizabeth that school time was close, nobody seemed much concerned with the approaching great event in my life. Instead, the talk of my parents after reading the daily paper was filled with strange words: *Serbia*, *Austria-Hungary*, and *Germany* and the *Kaiser* repeated over and over, but not so often as the one word *war*. I had heard enough old stories to understand what that word meant. I at last learned the German Kaiser was a man, and that the other names belonged to countries on the other side of the Atlantic Ocean. Still, these countries and England and France didn't look so far away on the map Mama showed me.

I forgot the war when one afternoon Elizabeth brought a letter from Granma Simpson saying she expected to visit us. We were not to go to any trouble for her; she would come on the afternoon stagecoach, visit with friends in Burnside until Papa had finished work, and come home with him. I regretted Elizabeth and I couldn't go meet the stagecoach.

Granma Simpson, compared to Granma Denney, had visited us very little. I remembered only that she was a small, blue-eyed, gray-haired old woman, nice to have around. Mama told us that she was much older than Granma Denney

View of Burnside before 1912. Large buildings in center house the Chicago Veneer Company.

All photographs courtesy of Mrs. Clifton Lewis Thompson, Jr.

Stagecoach ready to leave South Fork ferry. Matched horses, rather than unmatched mules, usually drew the stagecoach.

Empty log boom on South Fork.

View of Burnside from Bunker Hill. Cumberland Grocery is largest building in center foreground.

Seven Gables Hotel

and lived in the same Wayne County home in which she had spent all her married life, but was now too feeble to live alone; for the last several years her youngest daughter, Aunt Lucy, with her husband and a growing family had lived with her.

Granma Simpson came one evening with Papa before full dark when the whippoorwills had started calling. We ran down the hill to meet her. Then when she had rested a bit, we had supper together; later she insisted on rocking Lucy to sleep.

Granma Simpson didn't have the snap and sparkle of Granma Denney; she did not wear mitts or big black silk bonnets with flowing tails; she hadn't even had her ears pierced for earrings when she was a girl as had Granma Denney. She talked but little and told few stories; these were mostly of her days as a schoolgirl or when Papa was a boy. Still, I wished she would stay with us always; home seemed a happier place.

There was less war talk while she was there, though the war was getting worse. Germany had declared war on France; England had gone to war against Germany. German soldiers were invading and destroying Belgium. The daily paper was filled with stories and pictures of the evil ways of the Germans with the Belgian people. Mama said she thought the gruesome stories were all lies. She read the papers, but talked less of the war with Papa of evenings.

Granma didn't seem to enjoy listening to war talk. I didn't realize it then, but Granma Simpson already knew more than enough of war. She had married during the second year of The War and lived near the road to Albany on which bands of guerrillas came and went. They stopped often to plunder, burn, and kill. She had experienced much and seen and heard more of the guerrillas; yet she never talked of The War as did many others with only handed-down tales.

She did enjoy talking of her grandchildren and answering Papa's questions on the news she'd had in letters from his scattered sisters and his brother. One sister had with her husband and young children settled in Alberta, Canada. I liked to hear Granma tell of the descriptions my aunt had written of the hard winters in that province.

Granma was always wanting to help, but churning and taking care of Lucy were the only things Mama would let her do; if she peeled tomatoes or cucumbers for the table, Mama would, out of Granma's sight, examine the peeled vegetables to make certain all the peels were off. She had told us Granma Simpson couldn't see well enough to help with the cooking. She had been to the optician in Somerset, but he hadn't been able to fit her with glasses by which she could read. I think she had cataracts. She spent a good deal of time knitting, but now and then wished she could see to read, the only times I ever heard her wish for or complain of anything.

7

BURNSIDE SCHOOL

CARRYING A CRAMMED LUNCH BOX, a new pencil, and a "rough" tablet, I went to school with Elizabeth. We ran down the school path, jumping the limestone ledges below the house, and on down the grassy slope where large cedars grew. Here the path turned to take us through a clump of buckeyes growing on the rim of a canyonlike creek valley below us. The path steepened as it turned down past big beeches until, nearing the bottom, sycamores lifted their white arms above us. We crossed the creek on a causeway of flat rocks; then it was up again by a path as steep as the one we had come down.

We stopped climbing when the path ended by the stretch of Antioch Road that ran above the creek valley. We followed this road only a short distance before leaving it to turn right into a lane that led past the back lots of homes, with the graveyard on the other side, and soon the Holiness Church. We could now see the school building. The biggest crowd of children and what I took for grown-ups I had ever seen was overflowing the sidewalk in front of the school with more people running up from all directions.

We reached the sidewalk. I tried to stop to get a better look at a group of young women with dresses below their shoe tops and their hair pinned up with large flat bows in back; they were laughing and talking with some young men in long trousers. Elizabeth wouldn't let me stop. She was pulling me through the crowd when the last bell began to boom. Students not in line ran to get there. Elizabeth and I were bumped and shoved as she led me to a group of smaller children buzzing into line near the door; she then ran to her place.

The ringing stopped. Everybody was now so quiet I could still hear the hum of the bell when the double door opened. Several woman and a few men came out to stand by the lines of pupils; one of the women came to the head of our line, while a man stood alone on the steps—just, it seemed, to make certain we were all lined up two by two. I knew he was Professor McChesney, the principal.

He nodded to the woman at the head of our line. We then followed her through the door and to the first room on the right of a wide dim hall with other doors up and down it and a wide stairway near the end. The room we went into was big and sunny, with rows of desks and in front of these, the teacher's desk. The two sides of the room not filled with windows had blackboards all the way across, and near the tops of the blackboards were numbers and the alphabet.

Everybody had found a seat when the woman said that those who had brought lunches should put them on a shelf in the cloakroom and that beginning tomorrow we should put our lunches away before sitting down. She opened a door in a front corner of the room, and I went with two other girls and a boy who had brought lunches.

Our teacher, now sitting behind her desk, told us her name, Miss Rankin, and that all of us should learn each other's names; the best way to do this was for each of us, turn by turn, to stand up and tell our names.

Miss Rankin wrote each name on a card after she'd heard it. My turn came. Finished, I looked around more; after studying the different hair bows in front of me, I looked at the one row of seats between my row and the windows. I was surprised to see the seats there were much bigger than those in the other rows, but big as they were, they were not too big for the boys and girls sitting in them; some were bigger than Elizabeth, and she was upstairs in the fifth grade. I was wondering if the big pupils were in the wrong room when a clanging from the hall made me jump. Miss Rankin told us the hall buzzer meant we were to line up two by two for assembly upstairs; we were to walk quietly, sit quietly, and try to join in the singing. Another clanging soon came and we were on our way. The stairs were wide enough for two sets of twos, for marching up beside us were what I thought were the second-graders, while behind came the third- and fourth-graders.

Miss Rankin led us to the front row of seats in a big room which I later learned was two classrooms divided by folding doors that were opened for assembly. As soon as everybody was seated, Mr. McChesney introduced himself and all the teachers. After a few words of greeting, he introduced the speaker, the Reverend Somebody from one of the Burnside churches. Everybody laughed at a joke he told, but I don't remember it, anymore than his name or the passage he read from the Bible, or what he said when he prayed for us. He talked for quite a while after the prayer.

After the preacher finished, one of the teachers led us in singing while another played the piano. I was glad the first song was "My Country, 'Tis of Thee." I'd heard my father sing it many times; I liked its music and felt close to it because of the rocks and hills in it.

Songs finished, Mr. McChesney dismissed us after telling us to be certain and bring to school tomorrow morning all the textbooks and materials we needed.

Back in our room, Miss Rankin took a pointer and named the letters at the top of the blackboard. She then asked if any of us could take the pointer and do the same thing. Several of us raised our hands. I was both proud and relieved when my turn came for the pointer. I had been afraid I would be expected to read when I knew only a few words. Elizabeth could read when she started school.

Time for morning recess came. Miss Rankin told us to march quietly out and stay near the school building; the hand-bell she would ring at the end of recess didn't make a loud noise. I dreaded being outside with so many strange children.

I had seen a few in Sunday school but didn't know them very well, and anyhow I didn't know how to play any games except those I played at home or at Sunday school picnics.

Outside I learned that most of my class didn't know how to play either; a few boys were getting into a game of marbles, but most of us were just standing around when Miss Rankin came. Everybody played and had a good time in the game of cat and mouse she organized.

We were all working together on telling Miss Rankin the words printed in big letters on cards she was holding out one by one, when one of the bigger boys raised his hand. Miss Rankin nodded to him and he said, "May I pleased be excused?" That was what Elizabeth had told me to say when I had to go to the toilets in the basement. I hoped I could find them when my time came.

We had finished the cards and were copying letters from the blackboard when noon recess came. Miss Rankin told those who were going home for lunch to go quietly outside and straight home. Those who had brought lunches must go first to the basement and wash their hands; then they should get their lunches and go outside to eat. In bad weather we could eat inside the building, but today we could come inside only to put away our lunch boxes and get a drink. There was to be no running in and out of the building.

I followed two other girls down to the basement where there was a row of toilets each in a little stall with a door, and across from them a row of washbasins.

I wasn't hungry and I dreaded the long noon recess—an hour and a half for first- and second-graders. What would I do all that time? Elizabeth wouldn't get out until later, and when she did, she wouldn't want me tagging after her.

I ate lunch alone sitting on a rock under a tree. In a way it was nice to be alone after being with so many. My lunch was much the same as it would be until I started fixing my own: a hard-boiled egg, two split, buttered biscuits that only half covered the pieces of fried chicken between, a cucumber pickle, a ripe tomato, and more buttered biscuits with jelly or preserves between them. There was usually a bit of sweet—

gingerbread, black walnut cookies, or more rarely a slice of layer cake.

Later in the year, ham or sausage would replace the chicken, with an apple or an orange instead of the tomato.

I ate all I could, but the bigger part of the lunch was still there. I wondered what to do. I knew I was not to throw scraps on the ground to draw flies. On the other hand when I carried the uneaten food home, I would get a lot of questions on what was wrong with the food, why hadn't I eaten it, and didn't I know it was a sin to waste?

I was wondering how to solve this problem of extra food when more children came out of the school building. Among them was Elizabeth, who hunted me and wanted to know if I was making out all right, but then left to lunch with the girl who was with her. Soon the bigger children came out, followed by what I surmised were high school students.

The case of the extra food seemed hopeless, so I made a leisurely trip into the school to put away my lunch box, reinvestigate the basement washroom, and become acquainted with the drinking fountain in the hall.

Outside again, I noticed that few of the smaller children had returned from lunch, but some of the big boys were taking turns pitching a big ball into a basketlike thing on a pole. Basketball practice, I decided; Elizabeth had described the game to me. I watched them a few minutes, and then left to investigate the shouts coming from behind some trees past the upper end of the sidewalk. The big boys were playing baseball while the big girls in long dresses watched the game. The yells and cheers I'd heard had come from them. I stayed only a little while. I didn't know the reason for the yells—maybe people were cheering for the boy who caught a batted ball or for the one who ran around the bases without stumbling to break his bones on the many rocks in the field. I became aware that I was out of place among the grown girls and came away.

I wondered why so many of the older pupils brought their lunches. I soon learned that Burnside High School had students who came from Antioch, Bronston, Tateville, and further south, walking or riding several miles daily. A few boys came from the other side of the Cumberland, sometimes crossing in a skiff, other times walking the railroad bridge.

On returning from the baseball game, I saw the school grounds were filled with children back from lunches at home. Boys were kneeling by several rings to shoot marbles; two jumping ropes were going, one giving "hot pepper"; there was a long line of jacks players on the sidewalk, and somewhere close by a game of London bridge had begun. I forgot that in watching a girl jumping rope and acting out what she chanted:

> I touch my knee. I touch my toe.
> And round and round I go.

She had begun to act out another chant when a girl I didn't know invited me to come play a game of hide-and-seek. I went with several others down behind the Masonic Temple and felt at home when a bigger girl counted us out with a rhyme I knew. Hiding and sneaking in without being caught were fun. I was sorry when the bell rang. I hadn't had a chance to hide my eyes.

The first thing Miss Rankin did after we were seated was read a story. The stories she read or told were the best part of the day for me. Story finished, we worked again on telling her the words on cards she held up for us to see. Next, she'd point to a letter at the beginning of a word, and ask if anybody knew what it said. Most of the bigger boys could make the sound, and could, when asked, usually give words that began with the letter. I had learned enough from listening to them that by the time she pointed to an *s* I could raise my hand. I made the sound but, flustered at being called on, the only words I could think of were *sea*, *sun*, and *Simpson*.

Time for afternoon recess came. Miss Rankin did not come out, but one of the big girls organized a game of prisoner's base that kept us busy until the bell rang.

We spent most of the time after recess in copying numbers from the blackboard. Try as I would, mine looked to be no kin of those on the board, and I already knew their names. During this session, the most I learned was that sharpening a pencil on a contraption fastened to a windowsill was a pleasure.

School out for the day, I waited as directed for Elizabeth and solved the problem of the uneaten lunch while waiting. There was little left by the time she came. We then went downtown to buy our school supplies.

At home our mother was eager to hear how we had fared. I was trying to answer her question of what I had learned when I saw to my sorrow that Elizabeth was helping herself to a square of freshly baked gingerbread. I loved it, but now, I was so filled with my leftover lunch that I could only nibble at a small piece.

There was always something to snack on when Elizabeth and I came home from school. Beginning in the fall, after the sweet potatoes were well cured, sweet, and waxy, there was usually a pan of freshly baked ones, kept warm enough in the stove to melt the gob of butter we put in through a slit in one side. Usually in winter there was a pot of vegetable soup or pinto beans boiled with bacon keeping warm on a back burner, but these were too much trouble to eat.

Among my favorites, kept in the dining room press, were the half-moon fried pies dusted with sugar and cinnamon and filled with a sweetened and spiced sauce made from sun-dried apples. Stack pies made with the same filling were also good. We had no reason to be hungry between meals, but there seemed to be an opinion among our elders that three meals were not enough for growing children.

The problem of what to do with my leftover lunch disappeared during the second week of school after Mama told me there was no need for me to wait for Elizabeth when I knew the way home. There was a pen with two fattening pigs in one of the back lots that bordered the lane to school. The pigs gave grateful oinks for the leftover food. At home food left in our plates was not considered wasted; it went into the slop bucket and was then poured into the trough in the pigpen. I thus had not wasted.

The days sailed by as did the pages in our primer. We were soon reseated and divided into three groups. I was proud to be put in the first group with the big boys and girls and others who were farther along in the primer and able to count. The other groups studied the same things we did, but were behind the first group in reading and numbers. The first group was learning to write all numbers to one hundred and do simple addition and subtraction. Everybody worked together on the sounds of letters, moving tongues and lips as directed and then hunting words in our primers beginning with that particular letter.

However, school was not all work. Each morning and afternoon Miss Rankin read a story and then led us in singing on the days there was no assembly. I was no good at singing, but enjoyed it, especially rounds.

We often worked with stiff sheets of colored paper which I learned was called construction paper. We made, or tried to make, small homes, trees, animals, people, and other things for the sandbox. Miss Rankin taught us how to cut and paste the paper for chains to swing with paper lanterns of many colors across the windows.

Each season and holiday called for a different decoration. Halloween witches and jack-o-lanterns were soon on all the windows. These were as much fun to make as a real pumpkin jack-o-lantern at home.

One afternoon between Halloween and Thanksgiving, I went home to find Granma Denney, wearing her usual black-and-white costume with black mitts and a white ruffled apron sprigged with black. She was churning but stopped to take me on her lap to hear all about school. Finished with school, she asked how my Bible verses were coming along; remember, I was supposed to know all the Beatitudes before she came back. Could I say them now? I managed only to stumble and stutter through "Blessed are the peacemakers; for they shall be called the children of God."

Granma expressed some disappointment, but was forgiving and hopeful, promising that we would learn the Beatitudes and at least the Golden Rule before she left. I was glad when Elizabeth came and Granma's attention centered on her.

Finished with Elizabeth, Granma returned to her churning and Mama resumed talking of what she and Papa read about and talked of most these days—the war and the Germans. I tried to listen to that as little as possible. News of ships sunk by submarines gave me the shivers. To die by drowning and never see who sank your ship was horrible beyond belief.

At school I almost never heard talk of the war. During recess I learned more games from other children, and Sugarloaf Town became my favorite. I knew the Eenie-meenie counting out rhymes and Wire, briar, but one day I learned a new one:

> Engine, engine, number nine,
> Running on the Chicago line,
> When she's polished, how she shines,
> Engine, engine, number nine.
> O U T spells out on you.

I learned more verses for needle's eye and seldom felt as lonely as during the first days of school. One day one of my playmates told me she'd heard of a Burnside man who had found a mussel in Cumberland River with a pearl in it worth thirty or forty dollars. But she wasn't certain the story was true.

I didn't think a mussel pearl could be worth forty dollars, but one evening I told Papa what I had heard and asked him if it was true. He wasn't certain either but thought a large, pale-colored mussel pearl might be worth forty dollars. Most of the mussel pearls he had seen were dark and of different shapes, not round with the same light color and glow as oyster pearls.

No, we wouldn't go pearl hunting, but he did hope the man was well paid for the pearl he'd found. He spent days in a skiff gathering and shucking mussels and he'd work for weeks without finding a good-sized pearl, and the shells he shipped to a Louisville factory that made pearl buttons didn't bring a lot of money.

The wish to go pearl hunting vanished when the fall rains began. I had more than enough rain when walking to and from school. During bad weather we were permitted to eat lunch in our classrooms and spend the noon recess indoors if we wished. We were forbidden noisy or running games, but sometimes Miss Rankin would lead us in a quiet game we could all play from our seats. After Thanksgiving we spent the most of our bad-weather recess time making decorations for Christmas.

The whole class was to have a Christmas party shared with the second-graders and their teacher. Each pupil was to bring a small gift to place under the tree. The last school day before Christmas came, and we had our party with gifts, refreshments, and games. I especially enjoyed pin-the-tail-on-the-donkey.

There was one flaw in the Christmas party; the bigger boys and girls and a few others who had not been coming regularly since the rains began were not there. I told of their absence at the supper table that evening and wondered aloud how they would ever learn to read and write if they didn't come to school.

Our father shook his head over them, and said they might never be able to write anything except their names, but it wouldn't be all their fault; maybe their parents couldn't read and didn't care whether their children learned or not; or maybe the children who dropped out didn't have winter clothing because their parents, if both were living, had no money for clothes or a Christmas present, no matter how small.

Our mother said there was no need to worry about them; they were either white trash or their fathers used every cent they could get their hands on to get drunk.

Our father shook his head. The town drunk didn't have any children; the saloonkeepers ought to quit selling to him, but then he reckoned the man would buy moonshine; there was plenty of it around.

The new words interested me. I asked several questions: What was a town drunk? What was a saloon? Could I see one? Could you use moonshine for hot toddies the same as whiskey? All I received by way of answer came from my mother—a command to clear away some of the dirty dishes to make room for the cobbler pie Granma Denney had made.

At home Papa cut a little cedar tree, nice as the one we'd had last Christmas. We decorated it much as usual until just before the candles were lighted. Then Elizabeth and I went for the milkweed pods we had gather early in the fall when they were ready to burst. We had kept them dry, but closed, for the Christmas tree. We scattered the small seed with their downy wings all over the tree. In the candlelight the innumerable thin threads sparkled until the whole tree was aglow.

Christmas morning, I received among my other gifts a child's version of *Robinson Crusoe* which, with help from Granma Denney, I read during Christmas vacation.

Shortly afterward, I and others in the first two rows finished the primer and went on to the first reader. I don't recall the name of the book and remember only one story—the tale of Chicken Little who believed Foxy-Loxy when he said the sky was falling and ran to spread the news; Henny-Penny, Ducky-Lucky, Goosey-Lucy, and Turkey-Lurky heard and to be safe from the falling sky ran with Chicken Little into Foxy-Loxy's hole. I could imagine all got safely out.

We continued to work on our numbers, learning to read and write, from dictation, numbers above one hundred. Each day we practiced the sounds of certain letters, which I later learned were consonants, until Miss Rankin was satisfied we knew them. We then began practicing the sounds of a few combinations such as *st* and *tr*.

Early spring that year was saddened by Granma Denney's leaving when the dogwood and redbud were in bloom. A few days later, I became happier when after we in the first group had finished our first readers, Miss Rankin lent us other books to read. We had almost finished these books when it was time to take off our long underwear, and with it the long black stockings. I enjoyed the wind on my legs less than usual. The last day of school was getting close. That meant no more Miss Rankin.

I was also unhappy because of my grade in penmanship. All pupils received monthly report cards to be taken to our parents. My deportment, reading, and numbers had E's for excellence. Penmanship had brought only two VG's for very good, and these early in the year; a line of G's for good followed.

Mama never praised Elizabeth and me for the E's we made, but took them for granted. Elizabeth usually made all E's, even in penmanship and this in spite of having to work with her right hand when she had been born to use her left. Each time Mama had looked at my G she had said I must do better. Granma Denney had lectured me on the importance of fine penmanship for a lady.

My eighth and next-to-last report card brought another G for penmanship. Mama looked at it. Her mouth turned down; she told me that if my next and last report didn't have an E for penmanship, she'd "straighten me out." I knew what that meant, but try as I would, my penmanship did not improve.

My worries were momentarily forgotten a day or so before the end of school when Papa brought home news, not from the paper, but reported by telegraph; a German submarine had with no warning sunk the British ship *Lusitania*. More than a thousand had lost their lives; over a hundred of the dead were Americans. Mama said the Americans who were drowned ought not to have been on the ship; they had been warned and knew the seas around Great Britain were dangerous.

No need to quarrel at them, Papa said; they were dead.

We had a very quiet supper with little talk and were quieter than usual that evening.

The last day of school came with the last report card bringing another G in penmanship. All things: the drowned dead, Mama's future wrath at another G, my sorrow at telling Miss Rankin good-bye, were too much. I cried most of the way home and was still hiccuping and sobbing when I gave Mama my report card.

She thought I was crying just because of another low grade in penmanship. She comforted me with kind words and told me penmanship was less important than reading and arithmetic. Still she ended with the command that I should practice penmanship for an hour each day during the summer.

I wanted to improve my penmanship and did some practicing, but during the summer, home was its usual busy place, and I was busier than ever. Peggy was bigger and had more sense but still needed watching. Lucy was put under my care for what seemed hours at a time, and this kept me in or near the house. Now more than a year old, she had learned to walk during the winter and could be out of sight quick as our cat. I would find her climbing the stairs or off in the garden covered with loose dirt while trying to eat a raw beet or something else she had pulled.

My share of Lucy watching and other work was small compared to Elizabeth's. We both welcomed an errand to Burnside as a chance to get out from under. Mama had decided that since I was able to come home from school alone I could go downtown by myself. I went several times, usually all the way to the post office. I enjoyed the errands. I knew more people and more knew me; but no matter—people always spoke to each other. In Burnside nobody walked by anybody unnoticing as if the other were a piece of the sidewalk.

Joy of joys, one day after I had made two or three trips to the lower town with no mishaps, Mama suggested that on this trip I go to Mr. Matt Lloyd's store; his place was closer than the stores downtown if I took the path down and around the hill. I remembered, didn't I? She had brought me that way two or three times to look at the house while it was being built.

I remembered and set off down the hill following a path that led down and around to a stile over the railroad right-of-way fence. The railway curved out of sight southward, but looking in the other direction I could see down the glimmering rails to the tower where the freights sometimes took on water, and beyond, the Burnside passenger station.

I walked in that direction until I was on the gigantic fill that lifted the railway across the creek valley. There was room for my feet between the ends of the railway ties and the edge of the fill made of blasted-out rock that on my side sloped down to the upper lower town. I could see the road to Tateville, a few houses, and Matt Lloyd's store. I heard a northbound train whistle for the Tateville crossing. It was not far enough away to give me time to get off the fill. I learned that standing inches from a fast freight going by is no fun.

I turned back until I found a path going straight down the hill almost directly across from the stile. Mr. Lloyd's store itself was unchanged; the Indian heads were still in the window;

inside, the mixture of smells and varieties of merchandise were the same. The talk around the stove had changed; the men's voices were often loud as they argued about going to war.

I continued to enjoy the many trips to Mr. Lloyd's store or to the post office, but as the weather grew warmer, I began to feel the trip down was not worth the trip up. Going home, uphill most of the way, with the sun on my back and the groceries or dry goods I carried growing heavier and heavier, became pure misery; as time for the opening of school came closer, I was partly afraid of the second grade with a strange teacher, but I think that mostly I was glad to see the first day of school come.

8

MORE GREAT EVENTS

M Y REGRETS AT LOSING Miss Rankin were soon eased by adoration of Miss Vaught, teacher of the second grade. School had changed little from the preceding year. Mr. McChesney was still principal; assemblies continued with all the ministers of the town taking turns at praying for and talking to us. The same children played the same games in the same places on the playground. School had lost the excitement of my first year, but I still liked to go.

The only change I noticed was that the second grade was less crowded than the first had been; none of the bigger boys and girls I had known in the first grade were in the second, and several others were missing; there were also four or five pupils who had not been in the first grade. I wondered about this and asked Elizabeth. She explained that the strange pupils in the second grade had most likely been in that grade last year but hadn't passed; some of those I missed from the first grade hadn't passed; others had just dropped out; as you went higher in school there were fewer children in each grade. The fifth and sixth grades were so small they were together in one room with one teacher, as were the seventh and eighth.

Subjects in the second grade were the same as those in the first, except spelling. The class had written and oral spelling together. We still worked together on the sounds of letters, though we spent most of our time on combinations such as *at*, *st*, and *ing*, and soon we were asked to think of and write down our own "families." The *an* family, for example, would include *ran*, *pan*, *can*, and *man*.

For arithmetic and reading, we were divided into three groups, and once again I was in the first group. Addition and subtraction became more difficult; we learned the multiplication table through the nines and were soon able to multiply numbers above one hundred. Reading assignments were longer, and we began to memorize poetry. I remember best "My Shadow," "The Swing," and "The Wind."

Memory work for most of us seemed a natural thing. We had since babyhood been unconsciously remembering the names of our fingers (beginning with Thumbkin), games for our toes, handed-down riddles and Mother Goose verse, the songs and stories of our parents, and Bible verses for Sunday school.

My problem continued to be penmanship. We were supposed to make copies of printed matter with pen and ink. Great blots were now added to my undecipherable letters. I was afraid my grade would drop below a G and wondered fearfully what Mama would say—and do. Nothing happened. She had apparently given up my penmanship as a lost cause. I, too, more or less gave up and practiced only during penmanship periods at school; in my free time I joined with others in making decorations for Halloween, Thanksgiving, and Christmas. We had another Christmas party with the first grade.

At home on Christmas morning I found, along with another doll and the usual stuffed stocking, children's versions of *Swiss Family Robinson* and *Gulliver's Travels*. Elizabeth received more books than I, among them *Oliver Twist*—or at least I think that was the year she read the book aloud to me. I remember that as I listened I overflowed alternately with sympathy for young Oliver, hatred for his oppressors, terror of Sykes, and at last tears for poor misguided but good-hearted Nancy.

During the winter, the Christian Church was at last finished. A white frame building with no adornment except the spire, the church stood in a grove of trees in the upper

town on the same street as Dr. Stigall's office but on the opposite side. The double doors of the church opened into an anteroom that served as a cloakroom; it also had a bench where
mothers with crying babies could come sit until they were
quiet and then return to the service. All talk stopped when we
left the anteroom and went into the large room where services
were held. This too was plain, but the wainscoted walls were
of good hardwood that shone in the light from the tall windows.

We children followed Mama halfway down the aisle and
took our seats, while Papa went on to sit with the choir in one
corner of the elevated space for the pulpit; in front of the pulpit was the table with the communion service under a white
cloth.

Soon members of the choir were all in their places, Mrs.
Thomas on her piano stool, and the Sunday school superintendent rising from his seat to face the congregation. A hymn
followed the first prayer; next, the superintendent read a passage of scripture and talked of scriptural matters or Sunday
school business or both; after another hymn and prayer, we
went to our different classes. Only Peggy in the Beginners'
class could at that time go to a separate room in the corner
across from the choir. Other classes met in different parts of
the main room. Later, classrooms and a room in which an
older girl cared for the babies and young children were built in
the basement.

Class was for me the best part of Sunday school, especially
during the several years I was in Girls' Intermediate. I liked
my teachers. Mrs. Phillippi was a widow with a small son
younger than I. My other teacher, Mrs. Dick—for some reason we all called her Aunt Meg—was also a widow but older
than Mrs. Phillippi. Each week at home we studied the lesson
in the booklet provided us and memorized a Bible verse.

The two Burton girls, Jean and Kathy, were in the class and
our minister's daughter, Emma Bell, but the only classmate of
whom I stood in awe was Ella Mae Heath, the daughter and
granddaughter of steamboat captains.

Classes finished, we met again for more remarks from the

superintendent, prayer and more hymns. This was also the time for the birthday offerings, one penny for each year of age. There could be no cheating; at the appointed time the child walked to the front of the room and dropped the pennies one by one through a small slit in the top of the metal birthday box. The congregation could hear—and count—each clink of the falling pennies.

There came a Sunday when the superintendent announced the name of another "thoughtful child, only five years old" and made his usual speech of praise for the donor's thriftiness and charity, his words interspersed with apt scriptural quotations. He at last invited the little girl to come forward "to give your mite."

The congregation waited. Nobody came. Dead silence fell. Most were too polite to turn around and look at the red-faced, tearful child receiving nudges and soft hisses from her mother. It seemed a long while before the superintendent announced the next hymn. I later learned the girl had put the five pennies into her mouth ready for a quick grab and swallowed them all.

Sunday school was dismissed for Communion several minutes before church at eleven. This gave us children who had to stay for church an opportunity to go outdoors for a few minutes. Some of us would go down to the remains of the old academy below the church to look at the blackened blocks of stone and to walk along the edges of the crumbling basement walls and peer in.

The ringing of the church bell brought us back to the building in time to be settled for services. Church lasted an hour or better with most of the time given to the sermon. Lucy usually went to sleep. We three older ones were supposed to sit straight, with no twisting or turning to look around the room; we were to keep our glances on Reverend Bell and our minds on his sermon. Sitting still was easy; if I slouched or twisted my body around, the iron-hard starched points of Granma's knitted lace clawed at my armpits. I tried to listen, but spent more time in comparing the differences between male heads in front of me. Female heads were covered with hats. At home, Papa and Mama discussed the sermon over the dinner table with little help from Elizabeth and me. There were Sunday evening services also; Papa attended these alone until Elizabeth and I were a few years older.

Church in Burnside was not all Sunday school and sermons. There were Easter egg hunts, Sunday school picnics, class parties, and Christmas treats and programs in which we children took part. There were group activities for the young people—Christian Endeavor in our church. Most churches had a women's auxiliary that might plan a bake sale or bazaar to raise funds for the church, or gather to make clothing for the needy.

So far as I know, the first such organization in Burnside was the Women's Missionary Circle, organized by women of the Methodist Church shortly after the Methodists organized into a body back in the 1880s. Members of the Mission Circle helped organize the nondenominational Reading Club; there was also a Garden Club that for several years tried, with success in several places, to beautify Burnside. Later a Burnside Women's Club was organized and became affiliated with the Kentucky Federation of Women's Clubs. The Women's Club is of course nondenominational, but it grew out of the early organizations of church women, while the church auxiliary groups continued active also.

Still, the main purposes of the five Protestant churches in Burnside were to inculcate some denominational theology and lead their members toward a righteous way of life. Our church, different from many in the deeper hills, emphasized leading a "righteous life" here on earth more than the joys of heaven or the eternal fires and sulphurous fumes of the flaming pits of Hell.

There was agreement among all churches that breaking one of the Ten Commandments or a law of the land was a sin, but aside from this there was no general agreement on what constituted sin. One church permitted its members to dance; the closest thing to dancing we were allowed was a game of skip-to-my-Lou. On the other hand I can recall no member of our church who was stricken from the membership roll for playing in or watching a Sunday baseball game.

Burnside was a place in which man, woman, or child could walk alone and unafraid at any time of day or night. Mugging, vandalism, robbery—armed or unarmed—were unknown, as was rape. I think the churches perhaps had much to do with the safety of Burnside. Yet there was still sin in Burnside.

I heard often of men who had broken the Sixth Commandment. Only the town marshal or his deputy had the right to kill, if need be, but in a "shoot-out" the marshal was himself sometimes killed. I think it was during 1915 that the town had three different marshals within six weeks, though only two of these were killed; the third lived to quit his job.

Granma Denney had been pleased to learn I could recite the Beatitudes and the Lord's Prayer, but was scandalized when I could repeat only two, the shortest ones, of the Ten Commandments, and could get no further in the twenty-third Psalm than "green pastures." I went to work first on the Ten Commandments. I knew them by the time the church building was finished, but had not finished learning the twenty-third Psalm, though I often studied it under Granma's supervision when my after-school chores were finished. Studies stopped when Papa came home from work. We'd soon sit down to supper and everybody wanted to hear the news he brought.

Mama was more interested in the war and politics in Washington and Frankfort, which she could read about in the paper, but we children wanted to hear of Papa's day in the veneer mill, tides and booms in the rivers, and if East Burnside was growing into a town bigger than Burnside. Sometime after the South Fork bridge was finished in 1912, realtors bought from John Newell a large part of the floodplain of the South Fork across from Burnside, divided it into lots, and named it, in spite of its location, *East* Burnside. Several families had homes built there, but East Burnside was never anything more than a scattering of houses. Several times the residents had to flee from floods that carried away the South Fork bridge. The bridge was always rebuilt, but while this was being done, East Burnsiders could only reach Burnside by boat, usually a skiff.

I was more interested in the comings and goings of steamboats, and I pestered Papa with questions which he always answered. He in turn asked the same questions about school Granma and Mama asked, and one day in February, I brought great news home; the second grade was going to have a Valentine post office. We had already started decorating the box and were going to make valentines. Miss Vaught had said we could buy penny ones, but she thought it would be more fun to make them.

Two or three days later, Mama gave me twenty-five cents to spend for valentines, enough to buy penny valentines for most of my classmates. Unfortunately, I splurged, spending ten cents on a valentine for Miss Vaught. Still I felt the big thing filled with gold and scarlet hearts surrounded by lace was worth it. I wanted to give all the children in the room a valentine, and this meant I had to make so many, with help from Elizabeth, that we used all the square of red in my water-color box.

Valentine Day came, and the two boys chosen as postmen were busy delivering valentines from the overflowing box. Most of us had sent and in turn received many valentines.

The day after the party, Miss Vaught told us we should take the valentine decorations off the windows and start thinking of February 22. Did anyone know why we celebrated that day? Those who didn't soon learned it was the birthday of the Father of Our Country, George Washington. We heard stories of Washington as a boy, leader in the Revolution, and first president; then we made cutouts and drawings to illustrate the stories. At home Papa told us stories of the Revolution.

Easter was upon us almost before I knew it; I was trying on my new Sunday dress at home; Mama went to Somerset to buy a new hat for herself and straw hats with ribbons and streamers, and a rosebud here and there, for Elizabeth, Peggy, and me. Granma Denney had new head coverings from time to time, but they were always the same long-tailed black silk bonnets. I think this was the year Mama's Easter hat was small with the crown rising out of a bed of dark blue violets. Mama's hats, compared to most seen in church, were somewhat restrained. Sister Elizabeth remembers hats better than I: "Pigeon wings and peacock feathers did not appeal to my taste, but ostrich plumes sweeping over a hat or cascading to one side were something to see. I liked best those hats trimmed with little birds: sparrows, warblers, bluebirds."

Peg and I were less interested in hats than eggs. Day after day while I was gone to school, she looked into the hens' nests at intervals with the hope of finding a white egg. Most of our hens were Plymouth Rocks that laid pale brown eggs, but when time came to color them on the Saturday before Easter, we had more than two dozen; most were cream-colored instead of white but all colored well enough no hen could have recognized one as her own.

Easter came. Our celebration was the same as in other years; new clothing, special music and sermon at church, home to an unusually good dinner; then, weather permitting, Elizabeth, Peg, and I, after hurrying through the dinner dishes, were off to the egg hunt held by the church for its children.

Shortly before the end of school, Papa suggested that all of us go to at least one of the programs of the Burnside High School graduating class. Mama said she was feeling too poorly to go anywhere, but Papa could take Elizabeth and me.

We went to Commencement held in the evening at Masonic Hall, which would seat more people than any of the town's churches. We left quite early to be certain of a seat, but we found a crowd moving slowly up the steps, and when we at last got through the high double doors, most of the seats appeared to be filled. In time I learned that such crowds for high school graduations were the usual thing. Most Burnsiders were interested in the school; mill workers and owners alike sent their children as did several families in the surrounding country.

We eventually found seats where we could see the stage and after awhile watch the graduates march in from the back and take seats. I counted them but have forgotten the number; I think there were twelve. The girls were pretty in long white dresses and the boys handsome in suits and shirts with shiny stiff collars and cuffs.

The program included talks from two or three men and prayers from ministers, but I remember best the giving of the diplomas and listening to Mrs. Norman I. Taylor sing. I had heard people sing all my life, but had never heard anyone who could sing as she did.

Walking home by lantern light, Papa listened to my wonders and explained that Mrs. Taylor had an unusually good voice to begin with; and while she was still Mabel French, her parents had sent her to the Cincinnati Conservatory of Music where she had received a degree.

No, she was so far as he knew the only person in town with a degree in music, but not the only one with a college degree; her husband had a degree from Ohio Wesleyan, he thought, and there were others. Elizabeth reminded us that Mr. McChesney and the high school teachers had degrees, but they hadn't grown up in Burnside.

Whatever a degree was, I decided to get one—but not for teaching school.

Granma Denney had long since left us. The last day of school had come. My sorrow at leaving Miss Vaught was mixed with fear of Miss Lou Ballou, the third-grade teacher. From this year's third-graders I had heard of the paddle—"with a hole in it to make it hurt worse"—which she kept on her desk. Miss Ballou didn't just use that paddle on boys who threw paperwads or sailed airplanes and girls who whispered, but for not knowing your lessons. Spelling and arithmetic were hard, hard; I knew I'd get blisters on my bottom because of my penmanship. Worse, most of us had been told by our parents that whatever punishment we received at school for misbehavior would be doubled at home.

During the summer, thoughts of school behind or ahead of me were drowned in errands to town, churnings when the butter was too contrary to come though I churned so fast that clabber squished through the dasher hole, and feeding the stove, which during canning time ate wood like a Brobdingnagian. Any time left from these and other duties went to pulling weeds around flowers and vegetables.

A prayer one of the visiting ministers had recited in assembly kept running through my mind, though I tried to forget the hateful rhyme:

> Now I get me up to work
> I pray the Lord I may not shirk.
> If I should die before the night,
> I pray the Lord my work's all right.

Mama was feeling so poorly that Elizabeth had to do most of the cooking and help with the canning. It wasn't time for Granma Denney's return; I hoped Granma Simpson would come; she'd make Mama feel better and do the churnings. There was no more hope after Mama read aloud a letter from Papa's sister Aunt Lucy; Granma Simpson had grown too feeble to do any visiting.

A few days after we learned Granma Simpson couldn't visit us, Granma Denney came. We children were surprised. Here it was full summer, my eighth birthday only a few days past, and Granma had always come during the cooler fall weather. Mama showed only pleasure and chirked up considerably. Lately she had had no migraine attacks but spent most of her time, when not pressed by canning, in sit-down work such as sewing or crocheting and often lay in bed and read.

Granma Denney took over the churning, but nobody offered to help with my hardest chore—bringing the cow home to be milked. During the early spring, Mama had rented for cow pasture the overgrown fields belonging to the old couple around the hill. At first I had enjoyed the short walk along the lane to the pasture gate where the cow was always waiting. She'd run ahead of me, eager to feed her calf and bawling most of the way.

Shortly after the end of school, the calf was weaned and later sold. I felt sorry for the cow. During the first several days after the loss of her calf, she'd still be waiting at the lane gate, then run down the lane, and as she neared the barn she'd bawl for the calf that wasn't there.

My sympathy for the cow was added to sympathy for myself when she at last understood that her calf was gone. She no longer waited by the lane gate. Instead I had to go hunting her through sawbriars and gullies with never a tree for shade. She'd hide in the brush by a far fencerow and stand so still her bell didn't give one tinkle. Worse, when I tried to drive her, she wanted to go in every direction except toward our barn.

I forgot my troubles when we had a letter from Aunt Lizzie, Papa's sister and my favorite aunt, who lived in Somerset. All I remember of her letter is that she invited Elizabeth and me to visit her and Uncle Will during Pulaski County Fair week. We could go to the fair with her three girls still at home. That, I felt, would be the greatest imaginable treat.

Granma Denney spoke at once in favor of letting us go. Mama said she'd need us at home. Granma said she could do the work and look after Peggy and Lucy with no trouble. She brought up the matter during supper. Papa was all for our going; he said we'd worked hard and deserved the trip. Mama at last gave a reluctant consent. Elizabeth wrote Aunt Lizzie as soon as we'd finished the supper dishes. The fair was less than a week away.

I enjoyed the train ride; it was the beginning of a fine trip. The youngest of our three cousins, a little older than Elizabeth, met us at the Somerset railway station and took us home with her.

The afternoon was spent on a guided tour of Somerset. There were many stores and hotels and the courthouse, all crowded around or near the town square. Everybody seemed busy, going and coming on foot or in buggies and automobiles. I had never seen so many automobiles, not to mention people. Only a wagon of watermelons for sale was still; the seller had unhitched his team.

Our cousins took us through the courthouse and then out College Street to the high school. I was impressed not only by the school's size and the great trees around it, but also because I had heard it was among the best in the state. Back near the square we rested over ice cream in Guy Benelli's Ice Cream Parlor. I was intrigued by the pretty chairs with legs and little feet of twisted wire. Later at home Cousin Ida played the piano while the others sang. I remember the refrain of "Soldier, Soldier, Marry Me"—a song I heard then for the first time.

Yet, all these together could not compare with the Pulaski County Fair when county fairs were in their heyday. I think I spent most of the money Papa had given me on riding the merry-go-round and the Ferris wheel. I remember best the calliope, the bands, and the competition of the five-gaited saddle horses, all curried and combed until they shone like their polished saddles.

Elizabeth and I had so much to tell when we came home that we wore out Granma and Mama with listening, but Papa wanted to hear all about everything, especially Aunt Lizzie, Uncle Will, and the girls.

Coming home, I had hoped to find Mama in better health, but she was feeling as poorly as before we had gone to Somerset. A few days after the fair, Granma Denney gave Elizabeth, Peggy, and me an unusually early dinner, and then after hurrying us through the meal, she hurried us off to visit in a home down the hill. We were told to stay until somebody came for us. I have forgotten the family's name and think of their house as the Warwick Place, because Mr. and Mrs. Warwick later lived there for many years.

The children seemed to be expecting us; they met us at the gate and were glad to see us, but said we'd all have to play outdoors or in certain rooms. It was the day for the Ladies Aid to meet at their home.

The girls led us in an exploration of the big old house: the empty rooms, the porches upstairs and down, the kitchen, and at last the basement. Later I heard James Ballou had had the house built after selling his holdings in what was to be Burnside.

Members of the Ladies Aid came; the afternoon lengthened; the Ladies Aid left. My suspicions made the day seem long. Peggy cried to go home. Elizabeth reminded her we had to stay until we were sent for. The woman of the house comforted us with refreshments left from the Ladies Aid. Later, she invited us to supper.

Papa came as the first whippoorwills were calling. He told us we had a new baby sister. I felt sorry for Mama. Another girl! She had told me many times she wished I had been a boy, and when Lucy was beginning to walk and always getting into trouble, Mama would shake her head and say, "Pity she's not a boy."

Mama gave the new baby a long name, but we soon nick-named her Willie.

9

GRIEF AND GOOD-BYES

MAMA WAS STILL IN BED when school started, but feeling fine and counting the days until the required fourteen were ended and she could be up and about. All women around us were supposed to stay in bed for fourteen days after the coming of a new baby. I wondered why but never asked. Questions about a new baby brought ridiculous answers; a neighbor who came to visit Mama told me Mama had planted her toenails back in the woods and they had sprouted and grown into a baby.

I certainly would never ask Miss Lou Ballou about the how and why of babies. I saw the paddle, well polished and shining as if from much use, as I walked by her desk on the first day of school. Seated, I looked around enough to learn that not all the second-graders I had known were present; and several children who had been in the third grade last year were still here. Miss Ballou had failed them. I shivered at the thought.

I think that for the first several days we were the best-behaved class any school has ever known. No boy or girl whispered; the boys sat stiff and straight with no sprawling or sticking their feet into the aisles; no paper wads hit the blackboards or the ceiling; the pencil sharpener was not overworked.

We had a short morning recess, and only a "basement period" in the afternoon. We spent less time singing, listening to stories, or decorating the windows. We worked. I looked forward to reading and language, but I began to dread the other classes, even arithmetic. I didn't mind homework and seatwork. I feared being sent to the blackboard; it would go something like this:

"Harriette, go to the front blackboard! Now write, high as you can, nine hundred eighty-six thousand, seven hundred twenty-three. Multiply by eight thousand, seven hundred eighty-four."

The room would be silent, all eyes watching. Finished, I would turn around to face the class and hear: "Please, read your product."

I would struggle through the millions and eventually finish. Next: "Class, has Harriette made any mistakes?" If my answer was correct, I could take my seat; if not, I had to do the problem over again.

Fortunately, since all members of the class had to solve problems at the board, we had few turns at the blackboard.

Oral spelling, though I had spelled the words at home for Granma Denney, was still a terror. Each day some of us had to stand alone and spell the dozen or so words in the lesson. None of us knew when our turn would come.

One day a boy missed three words in a row. Miss Ballou laid him across her knees, and the paddle flashed through the air several times. I knew that sooner or later I would get it for penmanship. The first pages of my exercise book were too awful for anyone to see, especially Miss Ballou.

During penmanship practice, she walked slowly up and down the aisles, stopping now and then to watch.

The day came when, beginning in the back, she made a close examination of all in my row. She soon reached the pupil directly behind me. My work, if possible, grew worse. Ink from the overfull pen and cold sweat from my hand with drops from my chin mingled to flood the page. I had to get the sweat out of my eyes. Where was my handkerchief? Now I could feel her eyes on my moving hand; it poured out more sweat. I grabbed for the blotter just as she said: "Harriette."

"Yes, ma'am."

"Honey, don't be so nervous. You're gripping your pen too hard. You've smeared your face with ink. Go to the basement and wash your hands and face in cold water. Then, if you feel like it, go outside and walk around for a while. We'll try penmanship again tomorrow."

I loved Miss Ballou after that. My penmanship, with considerable help from her, did improve—somewhat.

Things at home were much the same. Our little sister Willie was growing. Granma Denney remained with us through the winter. Mama was eager as ever to read her magazines and the daily paper and then talk of what she read, not only of the war but also of who would be our next president—Woodrow Wilson for a second term or Charles Evans Hughes. I was glad when the presidential election was held shortly after Halloween; it would bring an end to the discussion.

But days passed while Papa and Mama wondered who had won. The counting of the votes was slow in some faraway state. Then one evening after supper we heard shotgun blasts, pistol shots, and yells from down in Burnside. "They've learned who won," Papa said.

We went to the front porch to listen, but there was little more to hear. Papa said Woodrow Wilson had won; the celebration was too small to be for Hughes in a place that was mostly Republican.

The war went on. My report cards were the same as those in the second grade with another subject, composition added. I got all E's except the G for penmanship. I was thankful to get that. Soon Elizabeth and I were busy getting ready for Christmas at Sunday school. Each day after school we went to church to practice Christmas songs and the pageant in which several children were taking part.

We were also having a White Christmas. This meant each member of a church family was to bring a gift of food or clothing wrapped in white tissue paper and place it under the church Christmas tree. The gifts would be distributed among the poor of the town. I wondered who the poor could be. I had heard Mama complain much of our poverty. I knew the owners of the mills and other businesses had more than we, but most men in the town worked as did Papa for day's wages, though we had some extra money from oil royalties. I had

108

noticed at school that a few girls wore hair ribbons little better than strings, and that in wet weather they didn't wear rubbers over their shoes. I couldn't blame them for that; I hated the things—hard to get on and off—but reckoned wearing rubbers was better than being like one girl whose shoes squished water when she walked. She stopped coming to school.

I felt our family was very poor only now and then when I had to wear one of Elizabeth's outgrown dresses; Mama had remade and retrimmed it, but the dress was still a hand-me-down.

I began to learn about poverty. One day when crossing the railway as I went to Mr. Lloyd's store, I passed on the north-bound tracks a man in ragged clothing who was picking up and putting into a sack the little pieces of coal that had fallen off coal cars. As the weather grew colder, I saw other men doing the same thing. I asked Papa about them; he said the men picked up coal because their families needed it for fuel.

My questions brought unsatisfactory answers. No, the men had no wood to cut. No, they had no money to buy wood or coal. No, the men I had seen picking up coal didn't have jobs; most likely they were too old or too sick to work at hard labor, the only thing they knew how to do. No, there were diseases like tuberculosis or a bad case of typhoid Dr. Stigall couldn't cure. Yes, Dr. Nick went first to the sick and thought of payment later.

The only help for people who couldn't pay came from neighbors, churches, and, in time of sickness, Dr. Stigall. He was out of his office much of the time traveling by buggy to reach a sick person miles away. He did everything from bringing babies to operating by lamplight, a dangerous business since the anesthetics then in use were highly flammable.

The hospitals closest to Burnside were in Lexington, ninety miles away. An ambulance to transport the dangerously ill to one of these was out of the question; had there been one available, the trip across the ferry and up the rough hill road would probably have killed the patient before he reached Somerset. Birth, illness, and death ordinarily took place in the home. At such times neighbors would bring cakes, pies, and other cooked foods, and help in any way they could. In cases of serious illness, neighbor women cared for sick women, and men stayed through the nights with sick men. Somebody, usually a young man, also sat with the dead at night.

The well-to-do would have an undertaker from Somerset, but before the Somerset-Burnside road was improved, the corpse remained at home until time for the funeral, always held for rich or poor in one of the churches, with graveside services later—long ones for the Freemasons. I know. Elizabeth and I were permitted to attend funerals. Paupers were buried in the back of the graveyard; such markers as they had were not visible from the road.

However, at home we were not thinking of the dying and the dead. Two or three days before our White Christmas, while waiting supper for Papa, Granma (who had already wrapped her gifts of mittens and socks she had knitted), was helping Mama wrap jars of jam, jelly, pickles, and preserves in white tissue paper while telling us of how when she was a girl people believed that on Old Christmas, cows and other farm animals knelt at midnight, but—

I heard no more of Old Christmas. Papa was coming through the door. Granma turned to shove a pan of biscuits into the oven; by the time Papa had washed and was sitting at the dining table the biscuits would be ready to serve, hot from the oven. Papa saw the jars Mama was wrapping, and, laughing a little, said: "I know one family that will have a fine Christmas; eighty dollars for a cow not worth fifteen, too old to calve and too thin to butcher."

Mama stopped her work to stare. "Eighty dollars for that worthless bag of bones. The railway people must be crazy."

I wished our cow would wander onto the railway tracks to be killed and we'd never buy another one. I knew it was hopeless; we lived too far from the railway, and anyway Mama would never do without a cow. I was back in the churning business; not long before Halloween Mama had told me I would have to go for milk and butter only a few more times; the cow had found a calf; she was giving lots of milk and we'd soon be using it.

During supper I asked so many questions that Mama at last reminded me of the cat I had grown to hate. How did the cow get on the railway when it was so well fenced? What kind of cow was worth so much money?

Later, I heard several stories of people who received unheard-of sums for worthless cows killed by trains, but I was never certain that any of the tales were true. In each story the Southern Railway outdid the Good Fairy. A brochure published in 1916 by the Burnside Commercial Club lists twelve lumber companies and eight other businesses and industries, not including the many retail stores in the town. Members of the Commercial Club did not say so, but if even half the tales were true the real bonanza of Burnside was the Southern Railway. The railway and other Burnside companies paid taxes, and each of the lumber mills used more local men as workers than the railway. Yet none of them accidentally killed worthless cows and paid ridiculously large sums for damages except the railway.

In spite of stout fence and cattle guards at all crossings, cows somehow got on the tracks to be killed. This happened almost every month. I heard whispered rumors that so-and-so had driven her old cow onto the tracks at night when she'd thought nobody was watching. I don't think all cows were killed through the trickery of their owners. Cows wandered all over, and after all, Old Sorghum, a dray horse, had managed to get onto the railway bridge, but was rescued. Still, it was strange that so many worthless cows got into the fenced railway right-of-way where there was little for them to eat.

I lost interest in the dead cows during the Christmas season. New Year's Day of 1917 came; we had used up all our sparklers and firecrackers, but I had not finished reading my Christmas books. Soon, it was back to Miss Lou Ballou; short division now, next fractions and more work in composition. The paddle continued active.

I learned more of Miss Ballou; she was a direct descendant of James Ballou, the first settler in what came to be Burnside. She was practically a neighbor, as she lived with her Ballou kin in Antioch and went back and forth to school on horseback.

She had been to college, and though she had not attended Burnside Wesleyan Academy, she seemed to follow that school's motto in her teaching: Thoroughness at All Costs.

There came a day in early April when school and spring seemed of little importance. The United States had declared war against Germany.

War or no war, we still had to learn our lessons during the few weeks left in the school term. Most of us passed into the fourth grade.

During the summer, home was its usual busy place with many chores for me—minding Willie, now able to crawl all over the house and trying to walk, and keeping three-year-old Lucy out of trouble added to my work.

Mixed in with talk at home of newspaper accounts of the usual bombing and submarine and trench warfare were new words: General Pershing, Flanders, Liberty bonds, and soon the words that frightened me most when I learned what they meant: selective service. I knew that Papa would have to go and be killed. He explained that unless the war went much worse than expected, the army wouldn't want a man over forty-five with five children.

Burnside grew busier than ever. The yard engine never seemed to stop hauling lumber and veneer to the railway siding. Chicago Veneer was cutting veneer to be used in airplanes needed for what everybody called "the war effort." Soon, Burnside store windows were filled with posters of Uncle Sam asking YOU to do this or that. Others pleaded in big letters: "MAKE THE WORLD SAFE FOR DEMOCRACY," while still others reminded us with pictures of red crosses and women in white that the Red Cross needed "YOUR HELP."

There was now on the main line little time between freights and the special passenger trains used for troops. The passengers—all men, sometimes in uniform, sometimes not—waved and called to me and others as we waited for the train to pass; some threw out letters and postcards to be mailed, or only slips of paper asking the finder to write to the name at the given address. I often felt like crying because near me I could see tears running down the faces of women as they watched the train go by.

I kept my sorrow to myself and never mentioned the weeping women around Mama. She seemed to feel more anger than sorrow over a war that took "our boys to fight in a foreign land." One evening in August she suddenly slammed down the newspaper she was reading and asked the air around her, "Now, why would they want to do a fool thing like that? There's plenty of sugar. Who is Herbert Hoover to tell me how much to use?"

Papa's effort at soothing her with the thought that the price of sugar and other commodities would be kept down failed. However, I heard little more of Herbert Hoover until weeks or months later when Mama filled out the family's ration coupons.

Meanwhile I had started to school and forgotten Herbert Hoover. I remember less of the fourth grade than of events at home during the year. I do know that Peggy started to school that fall and got along well with her studies and classmates. School for me under the young and beautiful Miss Amelia Saunders was not greatly different from last year. Miss Saunders used the paddle as much as or more than Miss Ballou did. The one to be punished was told to hold out his or her left hand, palm upward. Miss Saunders then gave the palm several smart licks with the paddle. I heard some of the punished say a paddle on your palm hurt much worse than a paddle on your bottom.

Granma Denney came as usual in mid-autumn. Soon, instead of lace, she was knitting woolen socks. I quarreled at the color, an ugly shade of brown. She explained she was knitting soldiers' socks; the Red Cross decided the size of thread and the color—khaki, to match the uniforms.

One evening when Mama had said something about the Massey Line Papa told her there was no longer a Massey Line. The packets and everything else Captain Massey and his partners owned had been sold for forty thousand dollars to the Cumberland Transportation Company. Mama sighed and said

113

she remembered seeing Captain Massey and his packets on the Cumberland when she was a schoolgirl.

Papa was more interested in oil than in steamboats. The price had gone up again, and his royalty checks were larger. In the early fall he'd told us that one of the drillers he had worked with in a Wayne County oil field was now manager of a new field opening in Wolfe County. Mama knew the man, Jeff Frogge, and many of his kin. They talked of him and wondered what life was like in Wolfe County.

I thought no more of the Wolfe County oil field. School work, chores at home, preparations for Christmas at school and at home with another White Christmas at church kept me busy. At times Christmas celebrations seemed wrong. The United States soldiers in the newspaper lists of war dead would have no Christmas.

It was only a few weeks after Christmas that Papa told us he had been offered a job as tool dresser in that new oil field in Wolfe County. The pay would be a great deal more than he was earning at the veneer mill. I could see he wanted to be back in an oil field. That evening after I was in bed upstairs, I could hear Papa and Mama talking; they seemed to be having a low-voiced argument. The only words I could catch were "school" and "Wolfe County."

I was home when he left on a Saturday within a week or so. I watched him go down the hill with a suitcase in either hand, and I heard him singing, "It's a long, long way to Tipperary."

Papa's absence left a hole nothing could fill. Elizabeth and I took turns going to the post office after school. His many letters helped. It was good to know he was getting along all right and liked his work. I found some consolation in writing to him. He somehow managed to read my miserable scrawls, for he always commented on what Elizabeth and I had written. Yet, all the letters in the world could not take his place.

Home seemed even lonelier when Granma Denney left in the spring. Elizabeth, Peggy, and I had to tell her good-bye as we left for school earlier than usual because we were carrying her bags to the railway station where she would take the motor coach to Monticello. Peggy cried all the way.

School was out for the summer. I had liked Miss Saunders—mostly, I think, because she had had us write many compositions; best of all, some could be imaginary. Still, I looked forward to being upstairs in the fifth grade.

During the summer I had among other duties at home to go daily to the post office, not in the cool of the day, but late in the afternoon when the sun had so heated the hill that it felt as if it would never again be cool. Mama wanted me to go at this time so as to get all the day's mail: "We might get a letter from your papa or your granma." She also wanted a newspaper with the late news; the Germans were pushing deeper into France; the daily lists of our war dead were longer. I heard and saw little in Burnside except talk and signs of the war.

One morning in June of 1918, Mama gave Elizabeth and me the job—ordinarily done in April and November—of taking the feathers out of the pillows used during the winter and putting them into clean ticks. We carried several pillows to a clean, grassy spot near the barn and went to work, ever mindful of Mama's commands not to let one goose feather escape and not to cut the ticking when we ripped the end of a pillow to be emptied. It was tedious work, but we at last finished the batch we had, hung the emptied ticks on the clothesline, and went to the house for more.

The upstairs bedroom windows were open, and we'd scarcely picked up a pillow when from the front yard we heard a strange cry and sobbing. Mama? I glanced out a window to see her halfway down the yard, and a man's back disappearing over the the hillside. Out of the house and closer, I heard her say between sobs, "I have no mother now."

That meant Granma Denney was dead. I couldn't believe it. Lucy and Peggy were standing by her, big-eyed and wondering, while Willie, now close to two years old, hung to the tail of her dress and cried. Elizabeth picked her up. Mama turned around at last and hurried to the house. She was soon ready to leave for Uncle Jack Denney's place where Granma had died. At times her sorrow changed into anger. She repeated, "Why, oh why, didn't they tell me Mother was on her deathbed."

She gave Elizabeth and me, especially Elizabeth, strict instructions on the care of the younger ones. We watched her hurry down the hill and continued to stand alternately crying and staring.

Elizabeth roused and went to the kitchen; the younger ones would soon be hungry. I made slow trips back and forth to the woodpile. It was not easy; one part of myself forcing the other part to believe I would never see Granma Denney again. I wished I could cry again.

Not long before suppertime Mrs. Charlie Miller, who lived in a new home down the hill with her husband and two children, brought us a basket filled with fried chicken and other cooked food. She asked Elizabeth if she knew how to milk. Elizabeth didn't. Mrs. Miller did the milking and strained the milk.

Next morning before we had finished breakfast, Miss Laura came; she'd only heard the news late yesterday; she took over the milking and stayed with us much of the time.

Mama was back within three or four days. She looked ready for death herself, or so I thought. Still, she kept busy in the house and garden. Neighbors and friends came to offer condolences. The Reverend Bell, our minister, and his wife also came as did Cousins Emma, Mollie, and Dora with Cousin Dora's husband, Preacher Taylor. I heard Mama bewailing Granma's "untimely, unexpected" death. Nobody knew her last words. She had died in her sleep after a day in which she had seemed well as usual, and only sixty-seven years old. Mama's grandfather, Jackson Denney, born in 1817, had lived to be eighty-three, while his wife, Jane Dick Denney, had died at eighty-six, It didn't seem fair. Mama was forgetting that Granma Denney had been born Harriette Le Grand Foster; she had lived with or among Denneys for forty-two years, but was, I thought, still Harriette Le Grand Foster when she died.

Home was a sad place; I looked forward to the beginning of school. During the first several days after Granma's death, a trip downtown was a reminder that Granma Denney was dead. I was thankful for Lloyd's store. The men around the cold stove talked of the war and the weather as they had for many months, nor did Mr. Lloyd remind me Granma Denney was dead. One day shortly before school was to begin, I heard a low-voiced argument over the disease that had killed a man. I heard one say, "Spanish influenza, I'm certain."

Spanish influenza? As I went home I chewed on the word, heard somewhere but still strange. I remembered at last, sometime back in the spring, Mama and Granma Denney had read a little about the disease in the paper. Granma had said that Spanish influenza was nothing but the grippe; anyhow it was in New York City—too far away to worry about.

Now men were thinking another man had died from influenza. That night after supper I read in the newspaper that several physicians were worried about a possible epidemic of Spanish influenza. The disease that had first appeared in the spring had reappeared in a more "virulent" form. I was uncertain of what *virulent* meant. I asked Elizabeth. She told me in whispers, after reading the paragraph, it meant that doctors couldn't cure Spanish influenza. It was killing people.

I understood. Yet on my trips downtown I heard less talk of influenza than of the war. Mama wasn't saying much about it as she worked on school dresses for the three of us. I didn't read the newspapers except to stare at the lists of war dead.

The opening bell for school rang on a bright September morning while I stood behind the barn and cried. Mama had decided we should stay at home because the Spanish influenza epidemic was spreading. No, we wouldn't get behind in our studies; she'd teach us at home. Staying home from school was harder for Elizabeth to take than for me. She had finished the eighth grade and was eager for high school. The afternoon of the second day of school Mama told Elizabeth and me to go to our teachers and Peggy's and get our textbook lists and buy what we needed on the way home from the post office.

She had said she would teach us. She did. Peg and I had a hard time. Mama felt Peg should have learned more arithmetic, spelling, and reading in the first grade. I had texts in Kentucky history, geography, language, arithmetic, reading, and spelling. Mama thought all were disgracefully easy for a ten-year-old. She bore down on arithmetic, grammar, and United

States history; for how, she said, could I understand Kentucky's history when I knew nothing of colonial days or the United States? She quizzed Elizabeth on American literature, had her memorize "Thanatopsis," helped her with algebra, and gave her many tests on Latin vocabularies and constructions. I noticed that in order to grade these she had to use the text. Mama often reminded me that Elizabeth, only two years and a few months older than I, was four grades ahead of me.

The days dragged on. The leaves as usual took on their bright fall colors to remind me that Granma Denney had always come in the fine fall weather like this. The gay reds and yellows of the maples seemed out of place when a church bell tolled—a sound we heard more often now. The leaves fell. From our house we could see the fresh mounds of red earth in the graveyard, and almost daily another was added. Many were for people who lived in Burnside; others were for those who had grown up in Burnside and then gone away.

Now, when I made my daily trips to town, people told me I should stay home so as not to "catch this flu." I heard worried talk of Dr. Nick; the only sleep he was getting was a wink or two when going to and from the sick in his buggy; and still many of his patients died.

Granma dead, Papa gone, the dead and dying in Burnside, the long lists of dead in the daily papers—my world seemed a place forgotten by God or could it be that God had died? I tried to put such a sinful thought out of my mind, and think of the one bright spot in my life; Papa told us in his letters that he was well and enjoying his work.

There was enough life left in Burnside to make a noisier celebration than the one we'd heard the previous fall when President Wilson was reelected. This time I asked no questions; I had heard and read enough of the race to know the racket meant Edwin P. Morrow, who lived in Somerset, had been elected governor of Kentucky.

It was little more than a week later while we were eating supper that the sounds of the biggest Burnside celebration I had ever heard came up to us. Added to the usual election celebration noise was the ringing of church bells, short happy rings instead of the mournful tolling that came so often. All the mill whistles were blowing; northbound trains blew continuously, southbound ones without much steam to spare gave quick, short whoops that matched the ringing church bells. The noise subsided at last, at least enough so that I could hear somebody down the hill banging a tin pan.

Mama said she was certain an armistice had been signed. She'd learned from the *Louisville Courier-Journal* that Germany was at the end of her rope, and an armistice on the Allies' terms was close. The news must have come by telegraph. The Germans were beaten; there would be no more killing, and our men would soon be coming home. I wanted to shout, bang a dishpan, do something. We ended by firing the twelve-gauge shotgun that made a big noise.

The celebration ended; the gray November days dragged on and church bells continued to toll often. December came; I remember nothing of Christmas. I think that because of the flu we had stopped going to church or Sunday school.

I have forgotten exactly when Mama made her Great Decision. She would sell the cow, fattening hogs, and chickens. We would then go live in the oil field with Papa at Torrent, Kentucky.

Papa came home to help with the moving. We were soon on the train to Lexington. Here we went to a different station and took another train that went past Winchester and on into the deeper hills to Torrent where we spent the remainder of the night in the town's one hotel. Shortly after breakfast next morning we left in a buckboard for the lease known as Bobbie's Ridge on which Papa worked. Getting out of Torrent meant a very slow ride. Located in a narrow, canyonlike valley with room only for buildings on either side, the one road was now choked, often to a standstill, by buckboards and mule-drawn wagons going in both directions. We were behind a wagon loaded with iron pipe and pulled by six mules. Leaving Torrent by a steep, uphill road, the horses hitched to our buckboard were restless because of the tedious pace; so was I. I couldn't blame our slowness on the heavily loaded wagon in front of us. Looking up the hill I could see other wagons equally slow, though teamsters beat their mules and the beasts in pulling stretched out until their bellies almost touched the mud and rocks underfoot.

Once we were on the sandy ridge road, the going was faster—except when we hit a deep chughole. The lease was only eight or ten miles from Torrent. We soon reached the lease where a scattering of new houses stood high on a pine ridge and the tops of drilling rigs showed here and there. The only location I can give for Bobbie's Ridge is something I learned from others; a few miles west of us there was a great natural bridge we ought to see; it was an amazing sight and within walking distance. The natural bridge of which they spoke was then unknown to the outside world; it is now Kentucky Natural Bridge State Park, easily reached by excellent roads.

Bobbie's Ridge was no kin of Burnside. I found it an exciting place of high, rock-walled ridges and narrow valleys. The ridges were covered mostly with pine, but there were trees and shrubs I had never seen; one of these was hemlock, which grew wherever there was a bit of earth at the foot of the cliffs. Spring brought many flowers new to me: first arbutus and two-colored birdfoot violets; soon, rhododendrons and mountain laurel; and later the great flowers of the giant magnolia that had leaves longer than I was tall.

Added to the excitement of a different world were the mystery of the busy drilling rigs and the pleasure of meeting other families. I usually went with Mama when she visited Mrs. Grover Foster, just beginning her family. Only a few years before she had been Sally Frogge in Wayne County. Mama was always eager to talk with anyone from Wayne County. I didn't know the people of whom they talked, and there were no children to play with, but I enjoyed being around Mrs. Foster. She was young and happy-seeming. Later, she and her husband bought a farm in Antioch where they brought up their sons.

Mrs. Foster never talked of the dangers for men working around us. There were accidents at various drilling rigs, and men were killed by the unexpected explosions of the natural gas that came from all the wells. The most dangerous work was hauling or mixing nitroglycerin; there were many stories of men blown to bits by the stuff. If a cartload blew, nothing was left but a wide hole in the road; horseflesh could not be distinguished from manflesh.

A name I often heard connected with this work was that of Harold Hardwick. He drove a nitroglycerin cart that went to many leases, including ours. Each time a well had been drilled, he brought the long tubes of nitroglycerin, lowered them gently into the well, then with everybody at a safe distance "set off" the nitroglycerin. We were sometimes permitted to stand a safe distance away and watch the oil shoot out, high above the drilling rig. This was done to shake up the oil in the rocks below and make it come into the well so that it could be pumped out. Harold Hardwick, only nineteen at the time, lived to return to Burnside, marry a Burnside girl, and achieve prosperity.

Life on Bobbie's Ridge was not all listening to talk of accidents and hunting lady's slippers or the white blackberries sometimes found in the creek valleys. Mama was an exacting teacher who never seemed to have heard of school vacations.

Sometime during the summer, she began to talk of sending Elizabeth and me to one of the small boarding schools twenty or thirty miles away. Mama visited the school and liked what she saw. Elizabeth and I were sent there at the beginning of the fall term. I think the place could have been called a cram school. Near the end of the nine-month term, I discovered I was about to finish the eighth grade to be ready for high school the following year. I didn't like the idea. Mama was pleased, reminding me I would be twelve years old before high school began, and that I was catching up with Elizabeth.

Elizabeth had enjoyed the cram school and returned the following year. My feelings for the place and for most of the teachers were far from love. The next fall I was a freshman at Stanton Academy, a Presbyterian school in the county seat of Powell County. I liked everything about this place and hoped I could finish high school there.

That was not to be. The school was getting ready for May Day festivities when I received a longer-than-usual letter from Mama. She told me to come home as soon as school was out; she would need me.

I further read that the Bobbie's Ridge lease was about drilled out, and since the price of oil had dropped to less than a dollar a barrel, no more leases would be opened. Papa's work would soon be finished; they would then move back to Burnside.

There was more in the letter, but I never read it. All the joy of the dance around the maypole was gone.

Our place on the hill was much as it had been: a large garden, cow and calf, chickens, and fattening pigs. Papa had done the work. Mama was feeling very poorly. I was no longer a child and saw, in spite of her loose voluminous clothing, that we could expect an addition to the family. Willie, the youngest, was five years old. I had thought there were as many of us as there would ever be.

Burnside had changed a bit. There were a few new homes near the Christian Church. The post office had been moved from low in the lower town and was now across from one side of the Seven Gables Hotel where Dick, Denney & Van Hook Dry Goods had once been. That building had burned, and after renting space in another building, the firm was having a new building constructed.

Moody's Dry Goods was a new store situated at the split in the road. The lower town near the meeting of the rivers seemed only somewhat less crowded than it had once been, but the biggest change of all was there: Chicago Veneer appeared much the same, but the company had changed hands and was now Burnside Veneer. The owners, Messrs. Gable and Glanton, lived in Burnside.

Everything else was much the same in the lower town. Most sales people and others I met greeted me with what appeared to be pleasure and told me they were glad the Simpsons had come home.

Such remarks surprised me. We had left in the winter of

1918–1919; now it was the summer of 1921. I felt so old, so changed during the almost three years I had been gone that it seemed strange anyone should recognize me. Somewhere, sometime, childhood had slipped away without my knowing.

The sixth and last baby came in July; when I learned the baby was a boy, I was certain Mama would be wild with joy. Yet when we children went in to see the new baby, Mama was doleful to the point of tears. A fine boy at last, she told us, but she doubted if she would ever live to see him grown. She hoped God would give her strength to live until he was a schoolboy.

We girls, thinking of her death, wept with her. We couldn't know that the baby would have long since grown to manhood when Mama died nearing eighty-seven years of age. It was Papa who died at fifty-eight when our brother was eight years old. His death was the direct result of an accident, though for years before he had been in poor health, his condition much worse than I then realized.

The new baby was named James William; each name had belonged to a grandfather. He received plenty of attention from his five sisters, the oldest fifteen years older than he, and the baby girl five.

I had more work to do at home than I had ever had, but my mind was often free to dread the beginning of school. The children I had known were now in the eighth grade. I wished I were there instead of a sophomore among strangers in high school. Elizabeth was eager to go. She would be in the same senior class she would have been in had she not left Burnside. At the cram school she had been able to finish three grades of high school within two years, making up the credits she had lost by studying at home.

The school had changed. Mr. McChesney was gone, but reminders of his plans remained: a machine shop for the boys had been built at the back of the school building, and the high attic was remodeled and furnished with the necessary equipment for teaching home economics. There was a class in agriculture, taught by one of the best teachers, or so I thought.

Styles in hairdos and clothing had changed. Most of the girls wore middies with skirts that a few years before would have been the subject of whispered gossip because they were indecently short. Several girls had short hair. The dangling sausages I had for years worn to school and brought home as tangled strings had been replaced by a long bob.

Customs at the school were much the same. High school girls went out to stand around the plot of ground that served as a baseball diamond. They invited me to come along. I usually did, though I often wished I could join in a game of jacks or sugarloaf town, or even jump rope.

I soon knew the other sophomores, at least by name, and began to feel more at home in Burnside High School; I even enjoyed the place most of the time. I especially liked the Literary Society. All high school students could belong if they wished, though by no means all attended the monthly meetings. Here we sang, or individual members gave readings or recitations which were later discussed. This part of the evening program was soon finished. The boys then shoved seats and tables against the walls. Soon everybody was in a game of skip-to-my-Lou and the fun went on and on. We never finished the song; somebody would always start a new verse, sometimes improvised on the spot.

None of the parents objected to skip-to-my-Lou. They considered it a game, not a dance. One evening at the Literary Society, some of the senior boys suggested we do the Virginia reel for a change. Everybody agreed; the boys chose partners, and while one of the girls played the piano, we bowed, twirled, and tripped up and down and around until late in the evening. Most of the parents would not have objected. Elizabeth and I knew how Mama felt about our dancing. Still, we and the others with like-minded parents didn't worry; this dancing was a school activity, and anyway who was there to tell them? Mama and others heard in the same mysterious way Burnsiders heard all things. We feared for the very existence of the Literary Society, but it survived.

It seemed only a short time until Elizabeth and her class were graduating from high school. Most of us at home attended all the functions. I remember little of the commencement exercises. I was deadened by the thought that within two years I would be sitting where Elizabeth sat now, and that within two years after that I would, according to Mama's plan, be ready to teach school. Most likely the only job a beginning teacher who knew nothing could get would be teaching all the grades in a one room school.

The following two years at home passed quickly. The next two years spent at Berea College didn't go so fast. I had chosen Berea mostly because that school required fewer hours of education for an elementary school teaching certificate than did the state's normal schools. This gave me an opportunity to take botany and geology as electives.

I earned the required certificate and taught two terms in the Pulaski County rural schools. Mama was pleased. I next attended the University of Louisville until I had earned a degree. Meanwhile, I had learned my future depended not on the plans of another, but on fate and myself.

Epilogue

NEVER AGAIN THOUGHT of Burnside as my home after leaving for school when I was sixteen years old. I visited home and later taught in the rural schools of Pulaski County. Still later, after marriage, I lived in the county for a few years, but not in Burnside.

I missed all the events that shaped life in Burnside. I only heard of the thousands of acres of cutover timberland in the county going into the Cumberland National Forest during the 1930s, and the news that U.S. 27 was at last paved all the way to Chattanooga came when I was far from Burnside. I wasn't there to hear the last whistle of a steamboat coming up the Cumberland.

The last Nashville-based boat to come to Burnside was the *Jo Horton Fall*, but she too was gone from the upper Cumberland by 1930. Burnside packets continued until around 1934, but for years before that, the few left were having difficulty in competing with the railways and the multitude of trucks that increased as roads were improved. Among the last of the Burnside packets were the *City of Burnside* and the *Rowena*, but both were sold before 1934 to become towboats. Log booms remained in both rivers, and launches owned by the Burnside Veneer Company continued to tow logs up the Cumberland. I don't know when the last stand of virgin timber was cut and the mills began on second growth.

I don't remember when I heard the last long whistle of a train. I discovered on a visit home that all the trains were diesel-powered; their whistles compared to those of the older steam engines were weak and somehow gasping. I don't know when the last passenger train stopped in Burnside. Now only freights pass on the Cincinnati to Chattanooga run.

I was in Pulaski County during the late thirties when work on Wolf Creek Dam began. The prospect of a dam to drown lower Burnside aroused little excitement at the time. World War II soon stopped the work. The Burnside Veneer Mill was for a second time producing veneer for warplanes, while most people had their young gone-to-war on their minds. I wasn't there when work was resumed on Wolf Creek Dam, and strange men, working for the army engineers, were up and down the Cumberland condemning land, some of which would later be sold for building sites along the lake. The veneer mill, the post office, the George P. Taylor Company, the Seven Gables, and other businesses remained in lower Burnside as long as possible. I wasn't there to see the wreckage and the moving. I didn't hear the dying sounds of Smith Shoals as the lake rose over the river and silently spread over the lower town.

Burnside, once Point Isabel, and further away in time a nameless piece of land at the meeting of the rivers, had long been giving the outside world what it needed or wanted; first the skins of beaver and deer, then farm produce, and at last timber. Now the world wanted electricity and recreation. This time the world took what it wanted.

Yet there is still a Burnside. The town is much smaller now, only a few hundred people. Many of these are descendants of the first settlers with the same names, but few are below middle age. There is little left to keep the young in Burnside.

A Note on Sources

JOURNALISTS AND POLITICAL or military historians wrote nothing of Old Burnside. I know of only one book that gives a good deal of space to one part of life in Burnside—*Steamboatin' on the Cumberland*, by the late Judge Byrd Douglas of Nashville (Nashville: Tennessee Book Co., 1961). I am grateful to the author's widow, Mary Stahlman Douglas, for permission to quote from this, the definitive work on the subject; packets owned and built by Burnsiders are included.

The first survey of the upper Cumberland and other materials were found in the archives of the Kentucky Historical Society. Pulaski County Court records and others records of the county yielded much information. I am indebted to the late Mrs. A. S. Frye of Somerset for the carefully researched records she gave me many years ago.

Much material on Old Burnside came from her residents—the living, the dead, and the gone-away. The Mabel French Taylor Collection of the Somerset Community College Library is rich in early photographs and other source material on early Burnside.

Papers of the late Nicholas D. Stigall contained many facts on early businesses, industries, and churches. Ms. Bernice Mitchell not only borrowed and copied these papers for me, but bolstered my memories and wrote to her brother Lindley for his boyhood memories of Burnside; Lindley Mitchell was most generous.

Ross Kreamer of Memphis, Tennessee, wrote of timber on the way to Burnside and sent photographs. Mrs. Baker Grissom, Sr., who continues to live in Burnside, was most helpful with her memories, photographs, and other material. Mrs.

Clifton L. Thompson, Jr., (Kathryn Gable) of Lexington contributed many early photographs as well as memories. Robert Taylor of Grosse Point, Michigan, gave me a good deal of material.

Others to whom I am grateful for their memories are Lonnie Bryant and Harold Hardwick who live in Burnside, and George Tuggle, president of the Pulaski County Historical Society, who lives near Burnside. Mrs. Henry Hail gave inspiration as well as information. Mrs. Hail, though now a widow, continues to live on the Waitsboro Road in a home built in 1836 and acquired by her ancestors in 1858. She was most generous with her time showing me over the house and telling the histories of her many antiques.